The Problem of the Criterion

Studies in Epistemology and Cognitive Theory
General Editor: Paul K. Moser, Loyola University of Chicago

A Useful Inheritance: Evolutionary Aspects of the Theory of Knowledge
  by Nicholas Rescher, University of Pittsburgh

Practical Reasoning: Goal-Driven, Knowledge-Based, Action-Guiding Argumentation
  by Douglas N. Walton, University of Winnipeg

Epistemology's Paradox: Is a Theory of Knowledge Possible?
  by Stephen Cade Hetherington, University of New South Wales

The Intellectual Virtues and the Life of the Mind: On the Place of the Virtues in Contemporary Epistemology
  by Jonathan L. Kvanvig, Texas A & M University

Blind Realism: An Essay on Human Knowledge and Natural Science
  by Robert Almeder, Georgia State University

Epistemic Virtue and Doxastic Responsibility
  by James A. Montmarquet, Tennessee State University

Rationality, Morality, and Self-Interest: Essays Honoring Mark Carl Overvold
  edited by John Heil, Davidson College

The Problem of the Criterion
  by Robert P. Amico, St. Bonaventure University

THE
PROBLEM
OF THE
CRITERION

Robert P. Amico

Rowman & Littlefield Publishers, Inc.

ROWMAN & LITTLEFIELD PUBLISHERS, INC.

Published in the United States of America
by Rowman & Littlefield Publishers, Inc.
4720 Boston Way, Lanham, Maryland 20706

Copyright © 1993 by Rowman & Littlefield Publishers, Inc.

First published in paperback in 1995 by Rowman & Littlefield Publishers, Inc.

All rights reserved. No part of this publication may
be reproduced, stored in a retrieval system, or transmitted
in any form or by any means, electronic, mechanical,
photocopying, recording, or otherwise, without the prior
permission of the publisher.

British Cataloging in Publication Information Available

Library of Congress Cataloging-in-Publication Data

Amico, Robert P.
The problem of the criterion / Robert P. Amico
p. cm.
Includes bibliographical references.
1. Criterion (Theory of knowledge) I. Title.
BD182.A45   1993
121′.65—dc20   92-37597
                                        CIP

ISBN 0-8476-7817-2 (cloth : alk. paper)
ISBN 0-8476-8034-7 (pbk.: alk. paper)
Printed in the United States of America

The paper used in this publication meets the minimum requirements of American National Standard for Information Sciences—Permanence of Paper for Printed Library Materials, ANSI Z39.48–1984.

To my parents
William and Marie Amico
and
my wife and best friend
Bonnie Jean Booman

Contents

List of Figures	ix
Preface and Acknowledgments	xi
Chapter 1: Introduction	1
Chapter 2: The History of the Problem of the Criterion	17
Chapter 3: Nicholas Rescher's Systems–Theoretic Approach	61
Chapter 4: Roderick Chisholm and the Problem of the Criterion	73
Chapter 5: Problems and Solutions	93
Chapter 6: Skepticism and the Problem of the Criterion	119
Chapter 7: Conclusion	143
Bibliography	145
Index	153
About the Author	157

List of Figures

Illustration 1. "Hands Drawing" by Jack Medoff	xii
1–1. Cube	4
5–1. Epistemic Map 1	95
5–2. Epistemic Map 2	97
6–1. Selection Task	135

Preface and Acknowledgments

This book offers a systematic historical treatment and analytic analysis of the problem of the criterion. My purpose is to show that there are at least two different versions of the problem, one posed by the Pyrrhonian skeptic, and one posed by the dogmatic skeptic. I offer a dissolution to both problems.

I argue that too little attention has been paid to the skeptic's position, and that the skeptic has been let off too easily in this historical debate. Consequently, I offer a critique of metaepistemological skepticism by showing it to be self-undermining. Such a critique sets the problem of deciding upon metacriteria of knowledge in a new light, free from the specter of skepticism. In the final chapter, I sketch an approach to this metaepistemological problem in terms of the shared presuppositions of the enquirers.

I would like to acknowledge and thank the many people who have helped me since I began this book. St. Bonaventure University provided me with a summer grant to work on completing the second chapter, and a sabbatic leave to finish my research. Theresa Shaffer gave me invaluable assistance in library searches and interlibrary loan services. I thank the many commentators and journal referees whose suggestions helped me to improve this work. Barry Gan assisted me with stylistic comments and Pat Dooley advised me on important details about publishing a book. I thank Earl Conee for his countless lucid, penetrating comments on earlier drafts. I am indebted to Richard Feldman for his clear and rigorous reviews of early and late drafts, and for his willingness to share his thoughts and friendship. I thank the referee of this manuscript, Paul Moser, for the pages of comments, which helped greatly in the final revision of this book. I want to extend a special thanks to Roderick M. Chisholm whose work on the problem of the criterion served to spark my interest in the problem and inspire me to write this book. Last, I thank my wife Bonnie for being my rock.

"Hands Drawing" by Jack Medoff

Chapter 1

Introduction

Philosophy begins with wonder. In this sense, we are all philosophers because it is our nature to wonder. Wonder brings questions, and these questions constitute a natural beginning to philosophy. Yet beginnings can be difficult and elusive, at least if we take the philosophical skeptic seriously. The skeptic would have us believe that we cannot begin at all, and this claim is the challenge posed by "the problem of the criterion." Before we can know just how seriously to take this skeptical claim, we must come to understand clearly the problem of the criterion.

Suppose you had a basket of apples and you wanted to sort out the good apples from the bad apples. It seems that you would need a criterion or standard by which you could sort them, either a criterion for recognizing good apples or a criterion for recognizing bad apples. But how could you ever tell whether your criterion for sorting apples was a good criterion, one that really selected out all and only the good ones or all and only the bad ones? It seems that in order to tell whether or not you have a good criterion, you need to know already which apples are good and which are bad; then you could test proposed criteria by their fidelity to this knowledge. But if you do not already know which apples are good and which are bad, how can you ever hope to sort them out correctly? And if you already know which are good and which are bad, by what criterion did you learn this?

This analogy is a paraphrase of Roderick Chisholm's explanation of the problem of the criterion, which itself was inspired by Descartes's reply to the seventh set of objections.[1] Chisholm claims that if we substitute beliefs for apples, we encounter the problem of the criterion—how do we decide which beliefs are "good" (actual cases of knowledge) and which beliefs are "bad" (not knowledge at all)? In the case of apples, there is no real difficulty because we already know the criteria for their goodness—firm, juicy, no worm holes or bruises, and so on; but in the case of beliefs, we do not. What is the correct criterion, method, or standard for picking out good beliefs or bad ones? It seems as if we need such a criterion or method for sorting out our beliefs. But how will we know whether or not we have the correct criterion, unless we already know some actual instances of good beliefs or bad ones so that we can check our proposed criterion against these known cases? So if we do not already know which beliefs are good ones and which are bad, how can we ever hope to sort them out correctly? How can we ever hope even to begin in epistemology?

The origin of this problem dates back to antiquity and the writings of Sextus Empiricus. It was a central issue in the debate between the Stoics and the Academic Skeptics. Interest in this problem surfaced again in the sixteenth century when Michael de Montaigne wrote his "Apology for Raymond Sebond" (1576). In the late nineteenth century, Cardinal D. J. Mercier brought attention back to the problem with his *Critèriologie* (1884). His pupil P. Coffey continued this tradition into the twentieth century with *A Theory of Knowledge* (1917). In this latter part of the twentieth century, two philosophers are responsible for the current revival of interest in the problem: Nicholas Rescher with *Primacy of Practice* and *Methodological Pragmatism* and Roderick Chisholm with *Theory of Knowledge*, *The Problem of the Criterion*, and *The Foundations of Knowing*.

With such a rich tradition in what appears to be one of the perennial problems of philosophy, one would not expect to find significant differences in the characterizations of the problem by different philosophers. Yet this is precisely what I have found, and it has led me to investigate the extent of these differences. I shall endeavor to show that even though these philosophers share common terminology, such as *the problem of the criterion* and the *wheel argument* or *diallelus*, and often cite each other's work, they are not all referring to the same problem. There are, in fact, at least two different "problems" of the criterion, one described by Sextus Empiricus and a different one described by Chisholm and Rescher. I will provide a historical analysis that will set each philosopher's discussion of the problem within its context and reveal the nature of each problem and the issues to which it is related. I will show how the proposed solutions of Mercier, Rescher, and Chisholm are inadequate and where their analyses, as well as Montaigne's analysis, are deficient. Also, I will offer a unique solution to each problem and demonstrate why the skeptic is wrong to claim that we cannot even begin in epistemology. This demonstration will mark a new beginning, a first step toward understanding.

PROBLEMS AND SOLUTIONS

By cutting the Gordian knot, Alexander found a quick and easy way to solve the frustrating problem posed by King Gordius of Phrygia. Unfortunately most philosophical problems are not dealt with so facilely, and this fact has led me to consider their nature more closely. What is a philosophical problem? What makes a problem a *problem*? What makes some problems only pseudoproblems? And when are two problems really *the same* problem? If we can find a way to answer these questions, then different problems of the criterion will be easily identifiable. An understanding of what a problem is will also shed light on what constitutes a resolution to a problem. Is there a difference between solving, resolving, and dissolving a problem? What conditions must be met to resolve a problem? To solve one? To dissolve one? When would a solution to one problem also be a solution to another problem? Nicholas Rescher purports to "meet and overcome"[2] the problem of the criterion, while Roderick Chisholm claims that "we can deal with the problem only by begging the question".[3] If we have a clear idea of what constitutes a solution to a problem, we will be better able to evaluate Rescher's claim and Chisholm's rather puzzling statement. The extent to which we rely upon these distinctions will be determined, in part, by how extensive or minimal the differences are between the various characterizations.

We can begin with a pretheoretical study of phenomena that count as problems and try to determine their common ground. Consider the following examples:

1. I need to get to Vermont to attend a wedding. My automobile is broken and I do not possess the knowledge to fix it. I cannot afford to purchase a plane, train, or bus ticket and know of no one going my way (we can suppose that the wedding is taking place in a very rural part of Vermont). Yet I need to be at that wedding because I am in the wedding party. It seems that I have a problem.

2. Imagine three perfect logicians, Moe, Larry, and Curly. Each could immediately deduce all the consequences of any set of premises. Each is aware that the other two are also perfect logicians. Moe, Larry, and Curly were shown seven colored hats: two red ones, two yellow ones, and three green ones. They were then blindfolded, and a hat from this collection was placed on each of their heads; the remaining four hats were placed in a drawer out of sight. When the blindfolds were removed, none could see his own hat. Moe was asked, "Do you know one color that you definitely do not have?" Moe replied, "No." Then Larry was asked the same question and he replied, "No." Is it possible, from this information, to deduce the color of Moe's hat, or of Larry's hat, or of Curly's hat?[4] This seems to be a problem.

3. In the following formula solve for x:

$$3x^2 + 14x - 12 = 57$$

This is a problem.

4   *Chapter One*

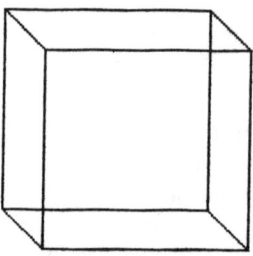

Figure 1–1. Cube

4. Consider Figure 1–1. Do we all see the same thing? Some people will see a cube viewed from a lower perspective, others a cube from a higher perspective, while others will simply see intersecting lines.[5] This is a problem.

5. Colonel Mustard was killed in the library with a dagger. There are no fingerprints on the murder weapon. There were five people in the house at the time of the murder, but only one had a motive: Mr. Peacock! But Mr. Peacock has a solid alibi. Who killed Colonel Mustard? This is a problem.

6. In the *Meno*, Socrates asks what virtue is, and claims not to know the answer. To this Meno asks; "How will you look for it, Socrates, when you do not know at all what it is? How will you aim to search for something you do not know at all? If you should meet with it, how will you know that this is the thing that you did not know?"[6] This again is a problem, and closer to the kind of problem that I am interested in analyzing.

What do these examples have in common? What makes such disparate phenomena problems? There is surprisingly little written about what makes a problem *a problem*. John Dewey describes a problem in terms of an *experienced* difficulty or perplexity: "[W]hatever . . . perplexes and challenges the mind so that it makes belief at all uncertain. . . ."[7] But this description is too vague to be useful in identifying and discriminating problems. Gene Agre claims that problems are undesirable difficult *situations*.[8] Agre's depiction is also too general and provides us no way to answer the questions we have set out to answer. For example, what makes one *situation* different from another? When are two people referring to the same situation? Agre's characterization gives us no way to make these judgments. Furthermore, his rendition is intended to pertain to every variety of problem, including practical problems, which makes it altogether too broad in its scope for our purposes.[9]

J. N. Hattiangadi offers an analysis of *intellectual* problems as logical inconsistencies.[10] This analysis rules out problems of the practical sort. A problem, by his account, is a set of statements that are logically inconsistent and that prompt one to attempt a resolution by making changes that yield a new, consistent set. A problem, then, brings with it the desiderata for its solution.

I find this part of Hattiangadi's analysis interesting and helpful, but he also denies that problems are questions and he denies that for a problem to be *a problem*, someone must be aware of it as a difficulty. I disagree with both of these claims and will explain why in what is to follow.

Harold I. Brown offers what I take to be one of the most important insights about problems: "Problems arise only in the context of presuppositions . . . which . . . provide criteria for the acceptability of proposed solutions."[11] Brown explains the importance of presuppositions in understanding what a problem is by citing the *Meno*. Socrates was perplexed by the question "What is virtue?" because he presupposed that virtue had a single essential nature that we could come to grasp. By Meno's initial answer to this question—explaining that virtue in a man is one thing, virtue in a woman is something else, and virtue in a child or slave is something other still—it seems clear that Meno did not share this presupposition and consequently did not view this question as perplexing or problematic. When he does come to share this presupposition with Socrates, the question becomes a problem for Meno.

To take an analogous example from teaching philosophy, I ask my students how many of them understand the nature of causation. Nearly every student's hand is raised. "What could be simpler than causation?" they think. To them the question "What is the nature of cause and effect?" is not a problem. They have not yet been exposed to the writings of Hume, Mill, Kant, and many others. But as a trained philosopher, steeped in the works of these philosophers, I find this question quite problematic. And this difference can be explained in terms of the shared or unshared context of presuppositions.

Uncovering the presuppositions of a problem, then, should also help to provide the desiderata for its solution. The presuppositions set the parameters for acceptable solutions. For example, Socrates' presupposition made Meno's initial answer unacceptable. Socrates tells Meno; "I seem to be in great luck, Meno; while I am looking for one virtue, I have found you to have a whole swarm of them."[12] But this answer is unacceptable because it conflicts with Socrates' presupposition that virtue has a single essential nature. This prompts Socrates to ask Meno; "Tell me, what is this very thing, Meno, in which they are all the same and do not differ from one another?"[13]

Although Brown does not offer a precise account of the nature of presupposition,[14] his thesis is consistent with Stalnaker's treatment of *pragmatic presupposition*.[15] Stalnaker's account is, in his own words, only a "sketch," but I believe that it will serve our purpose at this time. He characterizes presupposition as a propositional attitude or disposition of a person, usually exemplified by linguistic behavior. *People*, not sentences, make presuppositions.

> To presuppose a proposition in the pragmatic sense is to take its truth for granted, and to assume that others involved in the context do the same. . . . The

set of all the presuppositions made by a person in a given context determines a class of possible worlds, the ones consistent with all the presuppositions. This class sets the boundaries of the linguistic situation.[16]

My intent, at this time, is to offer a programmatic sketch of problems and solutions. This sketch will incorporate some of the insights from the scant number of sources I have found on this subject. They should be sufficient for my purposes in this inquiry. My precritical conception of a philosophical problem can be characterized as follows: Some of our intuitions are found to be mutually inconsistent when examined. Each, on its own, seems reasonable to accept, but together they cannot all be true. These intuitions can be understood in terms of an inconsistent set of individually reasonable beliefs.[17] For example, our intuitions about free will could be characterized as:

1. All events, including human actions, are causally determined.
2. Some human actions are done freely.
3. Statements 1 and 2 are incompatible.

Our intuitions about the issue of abortion are:

1. Babies are people.
2. Fertilized eggs are not people.
3. It is impossible to draw a nonarbitrary line in the development of babies from fertilized eggs that distinguishes persons from nonpersons.
4. Statements 1 and 2 and 3 are incompatible.[18]

Our intuitions about knowledge are:

1. People are capable of having knowledge about the world.
2. No one can be sure he or she is not being deceived about what he or she claims to know.
3. Statements 1 and 2 are incompatible.

Keith Campbell[19] explains the mind-body problem in terms of an inconsistent tetrad of propositions:

1. The human body is a material thing.
2. The human mind is a spiritual thing.
3. Mind and body interact.
4. Spirit and matter do not interact.

In the physical sciences, the same schema can be given to apparently anomalous observations:

1. Light behaves like a particle.
2. Light behaves like a wave.
3. Statements 1 and 2 are incompatible.

Since, in each case, all our intuitions cannot be true, the problem arises: which intuitions should we reject and which should we accept? Problems arise, then, quite naturally from a consideration of various propositions and how they fit into our body of beliefs. The kind of problems in which I am interested all have this feature and hence are to be distinguished from other kinds of problems, such as personal problems, financial problems, transportation problems, and medical problems. We might think of the latter types as practical problems of one sort or another and they will not be our concern.

This precritical conception of a philosophical problem fits nicely with the original meaning of the word "problem," which comes from the Greek *problema* (προβλημα), meaning shield, bulwark, hurdle, or impediment. The inconsistent set of individually reasonable propositions prompts one to question which one or ones are true and which are false. To correctly answer the question would, it seems, remove the "barrier," or problem.

Aristotle seems to have regarded problems as questions involving a conflict: "Problems also include questions in regard to which reasonings conflict (the difficulty then being whether so-and-so is so or not, *there being convincing arguments for both views*)."[20] Indeed, Aristotle wrote an entire book titled *Problemata* (Προβληματα), which is a series of questions that range from "How is it that one can become red in the face without perspiring?"[21] and "Why is it that, whereas we become wiser as we grow older, yet the younger we are the more easily we can learn?"[22] to "Why is it that some people, if they begin to read, are overcome by sleep even against their will, whereas others wishing to be overcome by sleep are kept awake by taking up a book?"[23] For Aristotle, not all questions are problems, only those that cause doubt: "For no one in his senses would . . . make a problem of what is obvious to everyone or to most people: for [it] *admits of no doubt*."[24]

Hence, a problem is always a question. A statement never poses a problem. For example, the statement "Knowledge is impossible" is not a problem, but rather simply a statement about the possibility of knowledge. If we then add the question "How, then, should we explain our intuition that we do indeed know many things?" we do seem to have a problem.

A problem should also be distinguished from a dilemma. A dilemma is a situation that requires a choice between equally undesirable alternatives. For example, suppose I am at the crossroads and need to get to London. Neither road seems desirable for that end. This situation poses a dilemma. Since a problem must be a question, a dilemma is not a problem. However, a problem can express a dilemma: "Which road should I take to get to London?"

A problem, being a question, always originates within a context of certain background assumptions or presuppositions. Sometimes these presuppositions are obvious. For example, in the question "Which road should I take to get to London?", I seem to be presupposing that there is a choice of roads. But many times it is not altogether clear what is being presupposed when someone poses a problem. For example, to the question "How is it that knowledge of the world is possible?", one might be presupposing that knowledge requires absolute certainty and that no one is absolutely certain of any empirical proposition; or one might instead be presupposing that the world is God and knowledge of God is impossible.

There are times when a person may utter a question and have no idea what he or she is presupposing or what would count as an acceptable answer. From the debate in 1948 between Bertrand Russell and F. C. Copleston about the existence of God[25] and the principle of sufficient reason, there emerged the question "Why is there any universe at all, rather than nothing at all?" It is difficult to understand what might count as an acceptable answer to such a question. This has led some philosophers, such as, Harold Brown, to identify these types of questions as pseudoproblems on the grounds that "those who utter them have no idea at all as to what might count as an acceptable answer so that all proposed answers are equally satisfactory and equally unsatisfactory."[26] I agree with Brown here because, if a problem always originates within a context of presuppositions, then if I pose a question where my presuppositions are unknown to me and/or not clearly conceived or well elaborated, then it will not be clear what kinds of statements are acceptable or unacceptable answers to my question.[27] Furthermore, I would add that questions that are, in principle, impossible to solve are also pseudoproblems. For example, the question "How do you square a circle?" is not a problem, because it is impossible to do so. This is, of course, just another way of saying that I have no rational doubt about how to answer the question. You cannot square a circle!

A problem is always a problem for a person at a time. Problems are relativized to individuals and times because they always imply rational doubt about the correct answer to the question posed. If I have no rational doubt about the answer to some question, then the question poses no problem for me at that time. From the examples cited earlier, it is clear that rational doubt arises because there are propositions that, although jointly incompatible, seem individually reasonable to accept for a person at a particular time. The fact that many people have had rational doubt about which propositions to accept and which to reject concerning free will or mind and body attests to our common experiences and explains our acceptance of them as perennial problems.[28] Relativizing problems to persons at particular times is consistent with our earlier claim that problems only emerge within a context of presuppositions and background assumptions and with the idea that by presupposition we mean Stalnaker's conception of pragmatic presupposition.

What do I mean by *rational doubt*? Let me stipulatively define *rational doubt* as:

> RD: S has rational doubt about P = def. S is more justified in withholding belief in P than in accepting P or rejecting P.

And to follow Roderick Chisholm's lead, let us say that "[a] person may be said to withhold a proposition P provided he does not believe P and does not believe the negation of P."[29]

What makes some problems distinctly philosophical is a difficult question to answer because it requires that in so doing we define "Philosophy." Since the point of this analysis does not turn on dealing with this issue, I am satisfied with a rather traditional response. Let us say that a philosophical problem is one that is in principle theoretical; one cannot decisively resolve it by empirical means, such as doing laboratory experiments and gathering data. For example, take the traditional mind-body problem and the inconsistent tetrad used by Campbell to characterize it.[30] And let us set aside, for the moment, the question of what pragmatic presuppositions I make in asking which proposition(s) I should accept and reject. No matter how much empirical evidence is collected about the brain and brain states, no empirical findings *could* ever *prove* that the mind is not a spiritual thing. It is, in principle, impossible to prove spiritualism false by empirical evidence. Hence, the mind-body problem (as characterized) is, in principle, theoretical, and in this sense all philosophical problems are theoretical.

This is contrasted with a nontheoretical, nonphilosophical question, such as whether the use of AZT is effective in treating the symptoms of AIDS. In this case, empirical evidence can be decisive in answering this question. This response differentiates philosophical problems from most scientific as well as personal or practical problems. I take these conditions to be necessary conditions for a philosophical problem but not sufficient. All philosophical problems must satisfy these conditions, but not all problems that satisfy these conditions will be philosophical. There may be problems in literary criticism, mathematical topology, and the like, which also satisfy these conditions. Also, there may be philosophical problems that are personal problems and practical problems as well. For example, the question "How should I live my life?"

may be all three. In order to give sufficient conditions for a philosophical problem, one would have to circumscribe that area of inquiry that is distinctly philosophical, and that task I cannot even attempt here.

Are there philosophical problems that can be decisively resolved by empirical means? Suppose I were a deterrence theorist who asks the question "Is capital punishment morally permissible?" And suppose that I presuppose that a punishment is morally justifiable if and only if it deters future commissions of the crime. Is this not a philosophical problem for me that can be decisively resolved by empirical means? I would argue that what is distinctly philosophical in the question is the presupposition concerning when a punishment is morally justifiable. This issue cannot be resolved decisively by gathering data and running experiments. But if we begin with this principle as a presupposition, then the remaining work is not really philosophical work. It is sociology. In recent years, the term "applied ethics" has been given to such investigations, and while they are quite valuable, I do not take such work to be strictly philosophical.[31]

Is there a difference between a pseudoproblem—one that is, in principle, impossible to solve—and a logical paradox, such as Russell's paradox or the liar paradox? Yes. A logical paradox is usually understood to comprise two inconsistent propositions to which one is led by seemingly sound arguments. Take, for example, the liar paradox. A person says, "I am lying." Is what she says true or false? It seems that if what she says is true, then she is lying and therefore what she says is false. Also it seems that if what she says is false, then she is not lying, which means what she says is true. Both lines of reasoning seem reasonable, yet each leads to contradiction.

I would say that insofar as a paradox involves rational doubt for a person (and having satisfied all other necessary conditions), it is a problem, not a pseudoproblem. However, if a paradox is, in principle, impossible to solve, then it is a pseudoproblem. Logical paradox is generally characterized a bit more narrowly than philosophical problems. Neither is a subset of the other, but they *may* share a good deal of common ground (where logical paradoxes meet the necessary conditions for philosophical problems outlined earlier).

A solution to a problem will always be a statement or series of statements. It must be a semantically appropriate response to the problem the question poses. For example, to the question "Who killed Colonel Mustard?", a semantically appropriate response might be "I do not know who killed Colonel Mustard." A semantically inappropriate response might be "The car is in the garage."

A solution to a problem must be an answer to the problem that the question poses. All answers will be semantically appropriate responses to questions but not all semantically appropriate responses will be answers to questions. I am relying here on a sense of difference that may be difficult to draw clearly, and an example may be helpful. To the question "Who killed Colonel Mustard?", one might reply, "Whoever shot the pistol killed Colonel Mustard."

The context here is important in determining whether this reply is an answer or simply a semantically appropriate response. The context reveals the presuppositions and background assumptions. If it is already presupposed that Colonel Mustard was shot with a pistol and that this shot was the cause of his death, but the perpetrator of the crime is unknown, then this response is no answer to the question asked. But we could imagine a situation in which this bit of information—that Colonel Mustard was killed by whoever shot the pistol—would enable us to deduce easily the identity of the murderer and solve the problem. In this case, such a response would be an answer to the question. However, not all answers to questions will be solutions to the problems posed by those questions. An answer to our question "Who killed Colonel Mustard?" might be "Mr. Peacock killed Colonel Mustard." Perhaps, however, it is perfectly obvious that Mr. Peacock could not have murdered Colonel Mustard. In this case, the response tells us something that was not already presupposed, but it happens to be false. Hence, every solution to a problem will be an answer to the question that poses it, but not every answer will be a solution.

A solution, then, must be true. There are no false solutions to problems, only correct ones, just as there is no false knowledge. Knowledge is always knowledge of the truth.

I take these conditions to be necessary but not sufficient for a solution to a problem. One other condition, I believe, will make them sufficient as well. Consider the following condition: A solution must remove rational doubt. If I no longer have rational doubt about which propositions to accept and reject, then the very cause of my problem to begin with (my rational doubt) has been removed. However, if an answer only gives me some rational grounds to prefer it over other considered answers, then this condition will not be sufficient for a solution to a problem. In such a case, it may be more reasonable to reject all the answers considered and search for a new answer.

To reiterate, then, a solution to a problem must be a true statement or true series of statements that is a semantically appropriate response, that answers the question, and removes rational doubt. With this characterization, I believe that I can now give identity conditions for problems in terms of pragmatic presuppositions and solutions. Consider the following identity principle:

> IP: X is the same problem as Y for S at T if and only if S makes the same pragmatic presuppositions in considering X as she does in considering Y and a solution to X for S at T is also a solution for S to Y at T and vice versa.

To use a simplistic example, suppose that we wanted to determine whether two questions posed the same problem: "How do you bisect a right angle?" and "How do you divide a 90-degree angle into two equal halves?" (Suppose for the sake of the argument that the two questions involve rational doubt for some person S at some time T.)[32] The answer here is that if S, who utters these questions, pragmatically presupposes the same propositions for each question, then since a solution to one question would be a solution to the other question for S at T, and vice versa, these two questions pose the same problem for S at T.

One of the shortcomings of Stalnaker's "sketch" of pragmatic presupposition is that a person can take any number of propositions for granted when asking a question, some of which might be totally unrelated to the question posed. Must not these propositions be related semantically or conceptually to the question in order to count as pragmatic presuppositions? How do we differentiate between those propositions that are related to one's question from those that are not? Perhaps we could formulate such a distinction for pragmatic presuppositions as follows:

> PP: Proposition P is a pragmatic presupposition of question Q for a person S at time T = def. S takes P at T to be semantically or conceptually related to Q in such a way that P constitutes at least part of the parameter or framework within which answers to Q count as acceptable kinds of answers.

For example, in the *Euthyphro*, Socrates asks Euthyphro, "What is piety?" Euthyphro promptly offers a list of pious actions in answer to the question. Socrates must then clarify his question by uncovering some of his pragmatic presuppositions, the most important of which is *that piety has a single essential definable nature*. Socrates takes this proposition to be semantically and conceptually related to his question in that it forms at least part of the framework for acceptable answers to it. By clarifying this pragmatic presupposition, Socrates is explaining to Euthyphro why his first answer is unacceptable and what kinds of answers will be acceptable—namely, ones that attempt to define piety as a single essential idea.

One might argue that if we identify problems at least in part by the pragmatic presuppositions a person makes in asking the question which poses the problem, then it is quite possible that two individuals arguing over the question "Is abortion morally permissible?" could be discussing different problems! One could be a Catholic ethicist and the other a utilitarian. They could presuppose quite different propositions to be true when they ask that question. For example, what it means for an action to be morally permissible for the Catholic will be different from what it means for the utilitarian. But then, it seems, they *are* arguing about different problems. One might be questioning whether abortion is against God's law while the other might be wondering whether abortion results in more or less utility. So I would agree that disagreements might sometimes look like they concern the same problem, when in fact they do not, and add that this characterization may help to explain why philosophers disagree so much and why settlement of such disagreements is difficult and rare. I am not suggesting that all disagreements stem from such factors, only that some may.[33]

One final consideration concerns whether we can distinguish between a solution and a dissolution of a problem. I believe that we can make such a distinction in terms of *how* rational doubt is removed. Suppose that you are asked, "How do you square a circle?" And suppose that you have rational doubt about the correct answer to this question because you take the question to mean "How do you construct a square equal in area to a circle?" Suppose that you do not know that such a problem is insoluble, that it simply cannot be done. You might spend a good deal of time trying to solve this. (I think Thomas Hobbes did!) It is a problem for you. Once you discovered this truth, however, your rational doubt would be removed by realizing the impossibility of the solution. I would call such realizations, which remove rational doubt, dissolutions. In a sense, one comes to realize that what one considered to be a problem is now only a pseudoproblem.

A dissolution of a problem shows a person who heretofore had rational doubt about the solution to a problem, that there is no longer any reason to doubt the impossibility of solving the problem. And hence the problem is no longer a problem. Suppose that the above question "How do you square a circle?" is understood to mean "How do you make a circle square?" There is no rational doubt about the answer to this question—you cannot! Such a question is not a problem for me.

A dissolution has the same effect. It shows us why we no longer have any rational grounds for doubting the correct answer to the question, because the question asks the impossible. I will reserve the term "solution" for those cases where doubt is removed by some positive answer. This would give solutions sole province over "real" problems. I shall use the term "resolution" to indicate either solutions or dissolutions.

Brown mentions another way in which rational doubt may be removed: "[W]e can reject a question by rejecting its presupposition."[34] By denying the presupposition made by the person posing the problem, the question loses its force because the rational doubt has been removed. To the question "Are you still robbing banks?", we can deny the implied presupposition that we have robbed banks in the past. I would call such rejection a *repudiation* of a problem. A "new" problem may arise involving the denied presupposition, but the original problem no longer exists for that person at that time.

I will employ these distinctions in my analyses of the various characterizations of the problem of the criterion that are to follow. Let us begin with the originator of the problem of the criterion, Sextus Empiricus, and follow with Michael de Montaigne and Cardinal D. J. Mercier.

NOTES

1. Roderick M. Chisholm, *The Foundations of Knowing* (Minneapolis: University of Minnesota Press, 1982), 63.
2. Nicholas Rescher, *Scepticism* (Totowa, N. J.: Rowman & Littlefield, 1980), 13.
3. Chisholm, *Foundations*, 75.
4. Adapted and paraphrased from Raymond Smullyan, *The Lady or the Tiger?* (New York: Knopf, 1983), 6.
5. This example is from N. R. Hanson, *Patterns of Discovery* (Cambridge: Cambridge University Press, 1958), 9.
6. Plato, *Meno*, 2d ed., tr. G. M. A. Grube (Indianapolis: Hackett, 1981), 13 (80d).
7. John Dewey, *How We Think* (Boston: Heath, 1910), 9.
8. Gene P. Agre, "The Concept of Problem," *Educational Studies* 13 (1982): 121–41. His complete analysis involves five necessary conditions, but it pertains to situations that are of no interest to us. For example, Agre discusses a person's having cancer as a problem.
9. Agre also discusses solutions to problems in "What Does It Mean to Solve Problems?" *Journal of Thought* 18 (1983): 92–104. It is also too general to be useful for our purposes.
10. J. N. Hattiangadi, "The Structure of Problems, Part I," *Philosophy of the Social Sciences* 8 (1978): 345–65; and "The Structure of Problems, Part II," *Philosophy of the Social Sciences* 9 (1979): 49–76.
11. Harold I. Brown, "Problem Changes in Science and Philosophy," *Metaphilosophy* 6, no. 2 (1975): 177.
12. Plato, *Meno*, 4 (72a).
13. Ibid., 5 (72c).
14. Brown cites his own "Paradigmatic Propositions," *American Philosophical Quarterly* 12, no. 1 (Jan. 1975): 85–90, for his analysis of presuppositions as "paradigmatic propositions." This analysis is loosely rendered and quite different from the standard accounts of presupposition given by Frege, Strawson, and Stalnaker. He offers, rather, an analysis of what he calls paradigmatic propositions partially in terms of presuppositions, but does not indicate precisely to what sense of presupposition he is referring.
15. See Robert C. Stalnaker, "Pragmatic Presuppositions," in *Semantics and Philosophy*, ed. M. Munitz and P. Unger (New York: New York University Press, 1974), 197–213; also "Pragmatics," in *The Philosophy of Language*, 2d ed., ed. A. P. Martinich (New York: Oxford University Press, 1990), 176–86; and "Presuppositions," *Journal of Philosophical Logic* 2 (1973): 447–57. For an excellent, comprehensive

review of the three main theories on the nature of presupposition, see Scott Soames, "Presupposition," in *Handbook of Philosophical Logic*, vol. 4 (Dordrecht, Holland: Reidel, 1989), 553–616.

16. Stalnaker, "Pragmatics," 180.

17. For a similar view, see Nicholas Rescher, "Philosophical Disagreement: An Essay Towards Orientational Pluralism in Metaphilosophy," *Review of Metaphysics*, 32 (1978): 217–51. One might question why mutual inconsistency is required. In correspondance, Paul Moser suggested that it may be enough to have a case where what is made probable by one intuition is made improbable by another intuition. But whatever is made probable by one intuition and improbable by another cannot be both true and false at the same time and in the same respect. So, it seems that we are still dealing with an inconsistency.

18. This is paraphrased from Joel Feinberg, ed., *The Problem of Abortion* (Belmont, Calif.: Wadsworth, 1984), 4.

19. Keith Campbell, *Body and Mind*, 2d ed. (Notre Dame: University of Notre Dame Press, 1984), 14.

20. Aristotle, *Topics*, Bk I, chap. 11, 104b, 13–15 in *The Basic Works of Aristotle*, ed. Richard McKeon (New York: Random House, 1941), 197; my emphasis.

21. Aristotle, *Problemata*, tr. E. S. Forester in *The Works of Aristotle*, vol. 7, ed. W. D. Ross (Oxford: Clarendon Press, 1927), 869a6.

22. Ibid., 955b5.

23. Ibid., 916b1.

24. Aristotle, *Topics*, 104a6; my emphasis.

25. The Third Program of the British Broadcasting Corp., 1948, cited in *Philosophical Problems and Arguments: An Introduction*, 3d. ed., ed. J. W. Cornman, K. Lehrer, and G. S. Pappas (New York: Macmillan, 1982), 224.

26. Brown, "Problem Changes," 182.

27. This means that it is possible for the same question to be posed in different situations where at one time it may be a pseudoquestion posing a psuedoproblem, yet at another time it may be a bona fide question posing a real problem. The difference lies in how well defined the presuppositions are in the context within which the question is posed.

28. I am using the term "perennial problem" loosely here, because strictly speaking, if problems are in part characterized in terms of pragmatic presuppositions, then perennial problems would have to be ones whose question prompts the same presuppositions in different people. I will say more about this shortly when identity conditions for problems are offered.

29. Roderick Chisholm, *Theory of Knowledge*, 3d. ed. (Englewood Cliffs, N. J.: Prentice-Hall, 1989), 8.

30. See p. 6 and note 19.

31. My thanks to A. Wade Davenport for bringing this matter to my attention at the spring 1992 Tri-State Philosophical Association meeting where a version of this chapter was presented as a paper.

32. For our purposes here, we can ignore the fact that these questions do not pose a philosophical problem.

33. My thanks to A. Wade Davenport for his input on this point.

34. Brown, "Problem Changes," 181.

Chapter 2

The History of the Problem of the Criterion

This chapter has a twofold purpose. First, I wish to present the views of Sextus Empiricus, Michael de Montaigne, and Cardinal D. J. Mercier on the problem of the criterion. These are the primary philosophers who can be credited with presenting or re-presenting this problem to the philosophical community and who, in a sense, have forced us to attempt to come to terms with it. Second, I intend to determine which accounts of the problem describe the same problem and which describe a different problem.

SEXTUS EMPIRICUS

The first recorded account of the problem of the criterion comes from Sextus Empiricus in his *Outlines of Pyrrhonism*.[1] There are two places in the *Outlines* where the problem is stated. The most succinct version occurs at PH 2.19–20, titled "Does a Criterion of Truth Really Exist?":

> This dispute, then, they will declare to be either capable or incapable of decision; and if they shall say it is incapable of decision, they will be granting on the spot the propriety of suspension of judgment, while if they say it admits of decision, let them tell us whereby it is to be decided, since we have no accepted criterion, and do not even know, but are still inquiring, whether any criterion exists. Besides, in order to decide the dispute which has arisen about the criterion, we must possess an accepted criterion by which we shall be able to judge the dispute; and in order to possess an accepted criterion, the dispute about the criterion must first be decided. And when the argument thus reduces itself to a form of circular reasoning the discovery of the criterion becomes impracticable, since we do not allow them to adopt a criterion by assumption, while if they offer to judge the criterion by a criterion we force them to a regress *ad infinitum*. And furthermore, since the demonstration requires a demonstrated criterion, while the criterion requires an approved demonstration, they are forced into circular reasoning.[2]

Sextus has characterized the problem of the criterion by means of an *argument* where there is a *dispute* concerning a criterion of truth. Before trying to state the problem in terms of an interrogative, let us look at his other characterization of the problem at PH 1.114–17:

> In another way, too, the disagreement of such impressions is incapable of settlement. For he who prefers one impression to another, or one "circumstance" to another, does so either uncritically and without proof or critically and with proof; but he can do this neither without these means (for then he would be discredited) nor with them. For if he is to pass judgment on the impressions he must certainly judge them by a criterion; this criterion, then, he will declare to be true, or else false. But if false, he will be discredited; whereas, if he shall declare it to be true, he will be stating that the criterion is true either without proof or with proof. But if without proof, he will be discredited; and if with proof, it will certainly be necessary for the proof also to be true, to avoid being discredited. Shall he, then, affirm the truth of the proof adopted to establish the criterion after having judged it or without judging it? If without judging it, he will be discredited; but if after judging, plainly he will say that he has judged it by a criterion; and of that criterion we shall ask for a proof, and of that proof again a criterion. For the proof always requires a criterion to confirm it, and the criterion also a proof to demonstrate its truth; and neither can a proof be sound without the previous existence of a true criterion nor can the criterion be true without the previous confirmation of the proof. So in this way both the criterion and the proof are involved in the circular process of reasoning. . . .[3]

One might think that this argument is significantly different from the first argument cited, that Sextus is simply arguing that we need a demonstrated criterion of truth in order to make a judgment between true and false impressions. But this interpretation would be misleading because it does not explain why we need a criterion of this very special kind (i.e., a criterion that is demonstrated by a proof that is already confirmed by an accepted criterion) to make such judgments. The reason we need such a criterion is to *settle the dispute* between those who judge certain impressions true or false and those who claim the opposite. Sextus is saying that only such a demonstration *could* settle the dispute. Now there may be other nonargumentative ways of "settling a dispute," for example, by physical threats, bribery, blackmail, or giving reasons that fall short of this demonstration, but it seems clear from the context that Sextus is speaking about settling a dispute by means of logic and argumentation.

This leads us to interpret the second argument like the first, making the same point about being incapable of settling the dispute. We can represent this as an argument as follows:

1. [SHOW] Disagreement between those who judge impressions is incapable of settlement.
2. A person who judges one impression true and another false does so either critically and with proof or uncritically and without proof.
3. But he can judge the impression in neither way without being discredited, because:

   a. If a person judges uncritically and without proof, then the opponent simply disagrees with the claim and no settlement has been achieved (he will be discredited).

   b. If a person judges critically, then a person must do so by a criterion of truth.

   c. The criterion of truth is either claimed to be true or false.

   d. If the criterion is claimed to be false, then no settlement has been achieved (he will be discredited).

   e. If the criterion is claimed to be true, then either the person has proof of the truth of the criterion or the person does not.

   f. If the person does not, then no settlement is achieved (he will be discredited).

   g. If the person does have a proof of the truth of the criterion, then the person claims the proof either true or false.

   h. If the person claims the proof is false, then no settlement is achieved (he will be discredited).

   i. If the person claims the proof is true, then the person has either judged it by a criterion of truth or the person has not.

   j. If the person has not, then no settlement is achieved (he will be discredited).

   k. If the person has judged it by a criterion, then the person claims the criterion either true or false.

   l. Same as (d), for the new criterion.

   m. Same as (e)—around and around in a vicious circle or an infinite regress (depending on whether the same criterion or a different one is used).

4. Since (a) through (m) leads us in a vicious circle or in an infinite regress, statement 3 is established.
5. Therefore, disagreement between those who judge impressions is incapable of settlement (by statements 2 and 3).

From this analysis, we can characterize the apparent point of the argument presented by Sextus Empiricus with the following statement: Settling a dispute between those who claim certain impressions true or false and those who disagree is impossible. This is not a claim about whether knowledge is possible or not, but rather seems to be about the impossibility of settling a dispute. The problem of the criterion is posed in the *dialectical context* of a dispute between those who claim the truth of some impression and those who deny its truth.[4] Strictly speaking, my formulation of the point of the argument does not describe a philosophical problem; it is a statement about the impossibility of settling a dispute. In order to be a philosophical problem, the point should be framed as a question, whose apparent possible solutions or answers all seem unsatisfactory. Hence, we might formulate Sextus's characterization of the problem of the criterion as:

> How do you settle the dispute between individuals who claim certain impressions true or false and those who disagree?

There are many questions worth asking about this characterization of the problem of the criterion:

1. What does Sextus mean by "impression"?
2. What does Sextus mean by "settling a dispute"? Does he mean a demonstrable validation of one side? How would that differ from knowing that we know the truth of that side? How does the claim that the dispute is impossible to settle differ from the claim that second order knowledge—knowledge of our knowledge—is impossible? Why will *only* such a criterion settle the dispute?
3. Under what conditions should we suspend judgment? At PH 2.19, Sextus speaks about the "*propriety* of suspension of judgment" (my emphasis). If we suspend judgment, are we still claiming that settlement is impossible (because the claim that settlement is impossible is certainly a judgment)? If we "should" suspend judgment, is it an epistemic "should"? A moral one? How does it arise?
4. Might Sextus's argument be self-refuting? In other words, if his conclusion is, in the relevant sense, an impression, then might his claim to the truth of his conclusion undermine his own argument?

In order to understand Sextus's characterization of the problem of the criterion, we need to be able to answer these questions, and this can best be done by explaining a bit of the history surrounding Pyrrhonian Skepticism. Due to the breadth of this task, the reader should keep in mind that we will only explain those aspects that are relevant to answering the questions posed above. This is not intended to be a complete account of Hellenistic philosophy or even epistemology during that time.

The history of Hellenistic philosophy includes an ongoing debate between the Stoics and the Skeptics concerning the possibility of knowledge—the

Stoics claiming that knowledge is attainable and the Skeptics attacking their position. Both were strongly influenced by Socrates' dialectical method. Socrates was continually searching for knowledge and showing others, through argument, that their claims to knowledge were unfounded. His claim to wisdom was that he did not delude himself into thinking that he knew things that he certainly did not know, that is, he was at least aware of his ignorance, while others were not aware of theirs.[5] The Stoics, however, thought that they could attain knowledge, and set out to show how such knowledge is attainable. The Skeptics' route was also to search for knowledge continually, but they endeavored to show, through the use of Socrates' dialectical method, the error of the Stoics' ways. Thus, we can understand the Skeptics' arguments within a dialectical context inherited from Socrates.[6] This point will become important for a later discussion. A brief synopsis of the Stoic position, then, will make the Skeptics' arguments more understandable.

STOICISM

Impressions are "thoughts which present themselves to the mind and which the mind either accepts or refuses to accept."[7] They have propositional content. The impressions of rational beings are called rational impressions. To accept such a rational impression is to believe "that the proposition which forms the content of the impression is true."[8] To refuse it is to suspend judgment. Thus, the Stoics thought of perception as a *mental act* in which we *assent* to an impression.[9] This is to be distinguished from the mere passive receiving of impressions. The former give us perceptions, while the latter simply awareness.

Human beings do not start out with rational impressions. They start out with irrational impressions, just like animals (i.e., mere sensory affections). But these irrational impressions in human beings, give rise to very simple concepts—colors, shapes, and such. With these simple concepts, human beings can then have rational impressions, which, in turn, will enable humans to have more complex concepts and more complex impressions. Also, there is more involved in a rational impression than simply its propositional content:

> We cannot identify an impression by just specifying the proposition it is a thought of. To have a rational impression is to think a certain proposition in a certain way. . . . For the same proposition may be thought in any number of ways, and depending on the way it is thought we get different kinds of impressions.[10]

Among these rational impressions are some about which we cannot be mistaken and which cannot fail to be true. Sextus describes these "cognitive impressions" or, as he calls them, "apprehensive presentations" as something "imprinted and impressed by a real object and in accordance with that object itself, and such as could not be produced by anything not real."[11]

When we assent to a cognitive impression, we "grasp" (*katalepsis*) the real object that causes the impression, that is, we grasp that which really is the case—that which actually *is*. A. A. Long describes this grasping thus: "We assent to the impressions [e.g.] *that* there really is a black dog which we see."[12]

There is a certain feature that is "imprinted" onto cognitive impressions such that we can recognize and identify them as such from this feature. This feature is simply the fact *that they can be grasped—that they are evident*, and we recognize this feature intuitively. The impression "reveals itself and its cause."[13] In this way, the cognitive impression we assent to guarantees the truth of the propositional content of that impression; it guarantees that there really is some actual object in the world that exactly corresponds to that impression.

Evidence is an *objective feature*, then, which we recognize intuitively, and which guarantees the truth of the impression. What, then, is the relationship between evidence and truth? A cognitive impression is true because the proposition, which is the content of the impression, is true. *How* the content is thought, then, is irrelevant to the truth of the impression. For example, I may think that this pen in my hand is blue when I look at the pen and have this impression or when I close my eyes and touch the pen. The propositional content of both impressions is the same (for the Stoics, anyhow), and thus, *how* the content is thought is irrelevant to its truth.[14] Evidence (or being evident) is, however, dependent on how the content is thought. The thought that this pen is blue when I look at it may very well be evident to me, but the same thought when closing my eyes will be nonevident to me. For the sake of simplicity, we will assume also that cognitive impressions are perceptual, even though the complete account is more complicated than this.[15] As Frede asserts:

> What makes a thought or an impression evident is that it is already part of the representation of the subject of the proposition that the predicate should be true of it and that the representation of the subject is entirely due to the subject itself.[16]

Therefore, a cognitive impression is true in virtue of its propositional content and not because it is evident; yet all evident impressions must have a propositional content that is true. Having cognitive impressions, then, is criterional of truth for the Stoics; cognitive impressions are those impressions that guarantee their own truthfulness. The Stoics believed that unless there were such self-guaranteeing impressions, there could be no ground for knowledge.[17] Thus, in modern philosophical parlance, the Stoics were foundationalists who believed that some kind of epistemic priority is necessary for knowledge to be possible. I will return to this theme later.

Naturally, the Stoics were attacked for this position, questioned on how they could be sure that any particular cognitive impression was indeed cognitive. This questioning led them to modify their position (later), adding a condition onto these cognitive impressions—that there be "no obstacle" to the impressions.[18] Obstacles, as Sextus describes them, are "external circumstances" that obstruct our recognition. Sextus offers an example of an external circumstance as:

> For there are times when an apprehensive presentation occurs, yet is improbable because of external circumstances . . . when, for instance, . . . Menelaus on his return from Troy beheld the true Helen at the house of Proteus, after leaving on his ship that image of her for which the ten years' war was waged, though he received a presentation which was imaged and imprinted from an existing object and in accordance with that object, he did not accept it as valid. So . . . these presentations, although they were apprehensive, yet had obstacles. . . . Menelaus also reflected that he had left Helen under guard in his ship and that it was not improbable that she who was discovered in Pharos might not be Helen but a phantom and supernatural.[19]

If this further condition is also met, then, as Sextus explains, the impression:

> being plainly evident and striking, lays hold of us, almost by the very hair, as they say, and drags us off to assent, needing nothing else to help it to be thus impressive or to suggest its superiority over others.[20]

This concession, it seems, turns out to be fatal for the Stoics, because they now have to explain how it is that we recognize when there are obstacles and when there are not. The idea of so-called self-guaranteeing impressions, then, loses its power to guarantee truth unless there is also a way to show how to recognize when there are obstacles and when there are not. The possibility of error is introduced with this concession. It seems that the Stoics believed that through practice, one could improve one's ability to recognize a clear and unobstructed impression.[21]

What, then, is knowledge for the Stoics? Earlier, we said that knowledge consists in grasping (*katalepsis*) a cognitive impression. This can now be made clearer by the Stoic threefold distinction between *knowledge, apprehension,* and *opinion*. As Sextus states in his discussion of knowledge, apprehension, and opinion:

> . . . and of these knowledge is the unerring and firm apprehension which is unalterable by reason, and opinion is weak and false assent, and apprehension is intermediate between these, being assent to an apprehensive presentation; and an apprehensive presentation, according to them, is one which is true of such a kind as to be incapable of becoming false.[22]

Knowledge and apprehension both involve cognitive impressions, but assent in the former case is "firm" while in the latter case it is not firm. What is the difference between firm and weak assent? It seems that in the case of weak assent, I will not be able steadfastly to maintain my position against all arguments.[23] This is a very strong condition of knowledge, because it claims, in effect, that, as A. A. Long says, "knowledge must be irrefutable [i.e., as Long interprets it] . . . its possessor can prove what he knows by means of propositions that are necessarily true."[24]

Thus, reason and logic are part of the notion of firm assent; firm assent requires *irrefutable provability*. If one has firm assent for an impression, then one knows a validating proof for it. There is a sense in which the rules of deductive logic determine whether some argument can alter my assent. If my assent is firm, then there is no argument, compatible with the rules of logic, that *can* alter my assent. We can state this as the Stoic thesis of irrefutable provability: S knows some proposition, belief, or impression (h) if S's assent to (h) is firm.[25] Thus, in Platonic terms, firm assent is its own "tether."

An interesting upshot of this view is that the Stoics apparently claimed that neither they nor anyone they knew were wise people (i.e., possessed knowledge), and so for all intents and purposes there is no knowledge.[26] They were simply trying to show that knowledge was attainable. The Skeptics' attack, then, will be an attack on that position,—the position that knowledge is attainable; and thus, no doubt, it will also be an attack on the foundation of this position, that is, on firm assent to a cognitive impression.

This completes the synopsis of the Stoic view. I will now turn my attention to the Skeptic's attack.

SKEPTICISM ACCORDING TO SEXTUS EMPIRICUS

As I stated earlier, both the Stoics and the Skeptics considered themselves disciples of Socrates. It is important, then, to understand the Skeptic's polemic as an extension of the Socratic method. Recall that Socrates never claimed any knowledge or expertise.[27] He set out to show that those who claim to possess knowledge are mistaken in their claim. Similarly, the Pyrrhonian Skeptic (such as Sextus, rather than the Academic Skeptic) made no claims to knowledge or any claims to any position on the subject.[28]

The Skeptic's strategy against the Stoic was to show, assuming the Stoic's background assumptions and logical methodology for the sake of argument, that the opponent's position either involved a contradiction or that there was an equally strong argument contradicting that position, and, furthermore, that the opponent could not argue successfully against this opposing position. The opponent's position is alterable by reason—it can be "shaken by argument."[29] Thus, the Skeptic's argument is not intended as a positive assertion of any thesis. The purpose of the argument is only to show that, given the opponent's own logic and position (for the sake of the argument), his thesis is alterable by reason (i.e., the opponent does not have firm assent and therefore does not possess knowledge). It does not show that knowledge is unattainable, only that the specific claim made by the opponent is not knowledge; it does not meet the opponent's standard for knowledge. Thus, the Skeptic maintains *no position* concerning the argument or the conclusion or the logic involved in the argument; the Skeptic uses them to show the inconsistency in the Stoic's own claim, or lack of firm assent on the Stoic's part, using the Stoic's very standards.

Actually, even this characterization is too dogmatic to be Pyrrhonian. The Skeptic would maintain that his argument against the Stoic merely tends to leave him, as Frede puts it, "with the impression that the Stoics have not successfully argued their case concerning the nature and attainability of knowledge."[30] The Skeptic would deny that his argument *establishes* that the Stoic's conclusion is false, or even that it rationally moves the Stoic, for that would be to take a position; and the Skeptic takes no position.[31] There is as much reason (or lack of reason) to accept the thesis as there is to reject it—a state of affairs that Sextus calls *equipollence* (*isosthenia*).[32] Sextus characterizes Skepticism as:

> . . . an ability, or mental attitude, which opposes appearances to judgments in any way whatsoever, with the result that, owing to the equipollence of the objects and reasons thus opposed, we are brought firstly to a state of mental suspense and next to a state of "unperturbedness" or quietude.[33]

This gives us an outline of the methodology of the skeptical attack. It begins with an argument (call it a contra-argument), which creates a conflict that is equipollent with the argument under attack (call it the proargument).

This equipollence makes the conflict *undecidable*—incapable of rational settlement—in which case, we suspend judgment (*epoche*) because we have no reason to prefer one to the other. This results, as a matter of contingent fact, in a state of unperturbedness or tranquility (*ataraxia*).[34]

The intention of the Pyrrhonian Skeptic is, therefore, to maintain no position. There are no principles of Skepticism. The Skeptic undermines the position of others without ever maintaining a position him/herself. This explains why Sextus refers to Skepticism as an "ability" or "mental attitude" as opposed to a "philosophy."[35]

Whether it is actually possible for the Skeptic to undermine the position of the Stoic without ever maintaining a position him/herself is the subject of considerable controversy.[36] We will consider this question, because of its obvious importance to our consideration of Sextus's characterization of the problem of the criterion, along with the other questions we posed earlier. Thus, before returning to Sextus's argument, let us address these questions. We can begin by explaining what Sextus means by an appearance or impression.

Impressions

The terms "appearance" and "impression" have various specialized meanings for contemporary philosophers, and their Greek predecessors may have meant something quite different. Let me begin with an excerpt from Sextus on appearances:

> Those who say that "the Skeptics abolish appearances," or phenomena, seem to me to be unacquainted with the statements of our School. For, as we said above, we do not overthrow the affective sense-impressions which induce our assent involuntarily; and these impressions are "the appearances." And when we question whether the underlying object is such as it appears, we grant the fact that it appears, and our doubt does not concern the appearance itself but the account given of that appearance—and that is a different thing from questioning the appearance itself. For example, honey appears to us to be sweet (and this we grant, for we perceive sweetness through the senses), but whether it is also sweet in its essence is for us a matter of doubt, since this is not an appearance but a judgment regarding the appearance.[37]

Sextus is acknowledging a distinction between how things appear to us and how they are in themselves (i.e., how they really are; what is really true). Truth refers to the real existence of things, *not to appearances.* Thus, for Sextus, doubt does not extend to appearances *and truth does not either.* To assert the truth of something is to assert something about its real existence.

This explains why we assent to honey appearing sweet to us, involuntarily; we cannot help how we are passively affected. For Sextus, the statement "Honey appears sweet to me now" is not a claim that has a truth value, nor is it an object of knowledge.[38] According to Sextus, such claims are "not open to question, [and] [c]onsequently, no one, I suppose, disputes that the underlying object has this or that appearance; the point in the dispute is whether the object is in reality such as it appears to be."[39] The point here is that since no objective claim is being made, the claim is not open to dispute; they are immune (*azetetos*) from inquiry. Only when we claim that "Honey *is* sweet" are we open to dispute, for only then are we making a claim that is true or false. This is a very important point, because the idea that "how things appear to us" could be a matter of truth and knowledge is a *post-Cartesian* notion with its earliest roots in the writings of St. Augustine.[40]

We can now see more clearly where the dispute arises between the Stoic and the Skeptic. On the one hand, the Stoics were claiming that there is a kind of appearance (impression, presentation) that carries with it its own distinctive mark (evidence), such that our firm assent to it guarantees the existence of the underlying object precisely as it appears to us, that is, it guarantees the truth of the existence claim, for example, that honey is sweet. On the other hand, there is the Skeptic who presents an argument against the truth claim, or judgment, for instance, that honey is sweet, and not against the mere avowal of how honey appears to me now.[41] The argument, if successful, runs counter to the Stoic's own standard that firm assent requires irrefutable provability, and thus demonstrates by the Stoic's own standards that his assent is alterable by reason and thus not firm.

This explanation of impressions, then, indicates that for the Stoics, rational and cognitive impressions are never of the "this-appears-so-and-so-to-me" kind, for that would suggest that appearances had propositional content and were thus true or false. Furthermore, it seems that the Stoics and Sextus used the terms "impression" or "apprehensive presentation" or "appearance" differently. For the Stoics, rational and cognitive impressions have propositional content and truth values. This means that for the Stoics, these impressions are of the form "X *is* Y" as opposed to "X appears Y to Z at T."

The Stoic's notion of irrational impressions does not involve concepts, for they indicate simple animal awareness prior to the development of concepts in humans.[42] Thus, an irrational impression seems quite different from Sextus's notion of appearance, which certainly does involve concepts. Sextus's use of "appearance" or "apprehensive presentation" or "phenomenon" or "impression" does not seem to have a Stoic counterpart.[43] An example of such an impression would be "This appears white to me now" or perhaps simply "This appears white." These impressions are not open to dispute, and not subject to truth values. Consequently, they are not objects of knowledge.[44]

Of course, this question (whether impressions can be the objects of knowledge) was not even raised at the time of Sextus. But, there is evidence that a Pyrrhonian Skeptic like Sextus would *deny* (undogmatically or nonassertively, of course) that we could be certain about our appearances;[45] and it is important to remember that the example "This appears white" is not considered a judgment at all. Thus, the question of its truth, or one's certainty of it, is not a question that is answerable. This is obviously what Naess means by saying, "If they [appearances] are beyond question, they are also beyond answer."[46]

One might, then, naturally ask: Does this mean that the impression "This appears white" has *no* propositional content? This is a difficult question to answer for Sextus, and I would think that the answer depends on how we characterize "propositional content." It does not have propositional content in the sense that the proposition reflects or represents a state of affairs that actually is the case. That would be the Stoic understanding of impression, and that is why such an account involves us in truth values for the propositions. I believe that, for Sextus, impressions have propositional content and that they involve concepts; however, the content does not represent what *is* but rather only what *appears to be*, and that is not a matter for truth or certainty or knowledge.[47]

Charlotte Stough's interpretation of "This appears white" as nonassertion would, I believe, be consistent with this. She supports her claim about how Sextus is using language in a special way (nonassertive) by citing Sextus:

> Sextus reinforces this point and goes one step further when he adds that the form of skeptic discourse is also interchangeable with various non-declarative modes of speech, such as the interrogative (PH 1.189) and imperative (PH 1.204), which are equally serviceable in revealing how something appears.[48]

Settling the Dispute

To address our second question—what does Sextus mean by "settling a dispute"?—let us return now to Sextus's argument. We can see from the very beginning of the argument that the Skeptic (at least provisionally, i.e., undogmatically, nonassertively) accepts the Stoic's condition on knowledge. Recall that the Stoic maintains that "firm assent" is necessary for knowledge; firm assent implies irrefutable provability. And irrefutable provability would settle a dispute because firm assent is "unalterable by reason."[49] There can be no dispute where there is no possibility of disagreement, and irrefutable provability means that there is no argument that can be a *reasoned disagreement*, that is, that can refute or call into question one's position.[50]

Sextus seems to accept the Stoic thesis about knowledge here and, through the Socratic method, presents an argument that does alter reason. Thus, if Sextus's argument is successful, it seems that the Stoic had a hand in the Stoic's own demise. This seems to be Sextus's point in the following: "No true presentation is found to be of such a kind as to be incapable of proving false, as is shown in many and various instances."[51]

To answer our second question, then, "settling the dispute" may be possible in more than one way, but it seems clear that Sextus accepted the "irrefutable provability" thesis as *a* way of settling the dispute (for an irrefutable proof would indeed settle the dispute; no one could rationally dispute it). We should remember that Sextus is not maintaining a position vis-à-vis settling the dispute, but merely showing that the Stoic's position, by Stoic reasoning, is called into question.

Thus, it would be unfair to criticize Sextus's argument on the grounds that there are other ways of settling the dispute, because this is not Sextus's assumption. His argument comes to this: If you (Stoics) claim that irrefutable provability ensures knowledge and thus will settle the dispute, and that your claim that, for instance, "X is P" is irrefutably provable, then, by your own standards and your own logic, I will show you that "X is P" is not irrefutably provable.

This method, then, does not question the Stoic's standard for settling the dispute, it calls into question whether any claim can meet this standard. His argument maintains that for the judgment "X is P" to be irrefutably provable, we need a criterion that picks out "X is P" as true. The criterion, however, requires proof to be irrefutably provable. Therefore, a dispute over the truth of "X is P" is not capable of settlement, that is, is not capable of being irrefutably proven. An evaluation of Sextus's argument will come only after we are clear about the answers to all of our questions, because only then can we offer a clear evaluation.

Suspension of Judgment

Our next question concerns the suspension of judgment. Under what conditions should we suspend judgment? And why? Sextus explains that when reasons for and against any particular judgment are equipollent (*isosthenia*) "we are brought firstly to a state of *mental suspense*" (*epoche*);[52] and this suspense "is a state of mental rest owing to which we neither deny nor affirm anything."[53] So, suspension of judgment is a state brought about by our inability to decide between two contradictory judgments with equally strong reasons for both judgments, that is, we have no reason to prefer one judgment over the other. Sextus explains this equipollence as:

> When we say "to every argument an equal argument is opposed," we mean "to every argument" that has been investigated by us, and the word "argument" we use not in its simple sense, but of that which establishes a point dogmatically (that is to say with reference to what is non-evident) and establishes it by any method, and not necessarily by means of premisses and a conclusion. We say "equal" with reference to credibility and incredibility, and we employ the word "opposed" in the general sense of "conflicting;" and we supply therewith in thought the phrase "as appears to me." So whenever I say "To every argument an equal argument is opposed," what I am virtually saying is "To every argument investigated by me which establishes a point dogmatically, which is equal to the first in credibility and incredibility"; so that the utterance of the phrase is not a piece of dogmatism, but the announcement of a human state of mind which is apparent to the person experiencing it.[54]

From this quotation, we can see that even the idea of equipollence is not a matter of objective fact or dogmatic determination. Sextus has no precise way of measuring the "weight" of one argument or dogmatic assertion against another; it is simply a matter of how they strike him at that time. Since no argument or dogmatic assertion appears "stronger" than any other, he is incapable of deciding on any one of them.[55] A judgment that *would* give us reason to prefer it over another is one that is irrefutably provable.

Now why is it that we should suspend judgment in such cases? If we suspend judgment, then we will avoid error. And in the Socratic tradition, the avoidance of error was certainly a sign of wisdom.[56] In suspending judgment, then, the Skeptic is not asserting that settlement is impossible. The Skeptic is also not maintaining the position that in cases of equipollence one should (in some epistemic sense) suspend judgment. If Sextus *were* to maintain a position, then he would thereby be committed to beliefs about what *is*. It is more accurate to say that due to the equipollence of these arguments or dogmatic assertions, Sextus is unable to make a reasoned decision, based on the very standards for reasoned decision that the Stoics maintain.

Self-Refutation

Our fourth question concerns whether Sextus's argument against the criterion of truth might in some way be self-refuting. The simple answer to this question is "yes." Indeed, this is a feature that Sextus embraces and which is the hallmark of Pyrrhonian Skepticism. In a well-known passage, Sextus explains how his argument against proof refutes itself as well:

Just as, for example, fire after consuming the fuel destroys also itself, and like as purgatives after driving the fluids out of the bodies expel themselves as well, so too the argument against proof, after abolishing every proof, can cancel itself also. And again, just as it is not impossible for the man who has ascended to a high place by a ladder to overturn the ladder with his foot after his ascent, so also it is not unlikely that the Skeptic after he has arrived at the demonstration of his thesis by means of the argument proving the non-existence of proof, as it were by a step-ladder should then abolish this very argument.[57]

Thus, there is a sense in which Sextus welcomes the charge of self-refutation.

However, there is a sense of self-refutation that was charged by the Stoics against the Skeptics, that Sextus is keen to deny. Concerning the criterion of truth, Sextus relates their charge at M 7.440:

> But the Dogmatists [Stoics] are accustomed to retort by inquiring "How ever does the Skeptic show that there is no criterion? For he asserts this either without judging or with the help of a criterion; but if it is without judging, he will not be trusted, while if it is with a criterion, he will be self-refuted, and while asserting that there is no criterion he will agree to adopt a criterion in order to confirm that assertion."

If this argument against the Skeptic is telling, then it is quite significant for the problem of the criterion that Sextus has presented; if Sextus's argument is presented uncritically, he will be "discredited," and if he has employed a criterion, then his argument refutes itself (and again he is "discredited"). Hence, the "problem" will also vanish.[58] We must, then, look more closely at the Stoic argument against Sextus, and at Sextus's reply.

The Stoic's Argument

In what sense are the Stoics saying that Sextus's argument is self-refuting? Sextus characterizes self-refutation with the term "peritrope," or reversal. Burnyeat rightly points out that peritrope can mean several different things.[59] For example, *pragmatic self-refutation* "occurs if a proposition is falsified by the particular way it happens to be presented, as when I write that I am not writing—if I write it, it must be false."[60] It is this sense of self-refutation that Burnyeat maintains the Stoics have charged Sextus with in the passage cited above (M 7.440).[61] In other words, what Sextus *says* against the criterion of truth is falsified by his *saying* it. And if this were true, it would spell trouble for his characterization of the problem of the criterion.[62]

Sextus's Response

Sextus's reply to this charge of pragmatic self-refutation is to explain that when he presents an argument against the criterion of truth, which is what the

Stoics must deal with, he is not himself assenting to it or its conclusion (i.e., he is not asserting it dogmatically). He is merely explaining how things *appear* to him, and such utterances (as we have learned from our previous discussion on impressions) do not have truth values. And if his utterances do not make assertions that have truth values, then they cannot possibly be self-refuting in *any* way. Nonetheless, his impression of his presentation of the argument against the Stoic criterion and the Stoic's argument in favor of it seem equally probable and, hence, he is led to suspend judgment on the matter, being unable to decide between the two.[63] If Sextus is correct, then his problem of the criterion has been saved from obliteration.

Burnyeat seems to side with the Stoics on this matter when he avers:

> Reason-giving is not just another independent activity alongside the advancing of views, since a relation and reference to each other is part of our understanding both of what a reason is and of what it is to hold a view. . . . And however we express the point, this is something that deserves to be called self-refuting. A man who cites a reason why no reason can be given for anything seems both to do and to acknowledge that he is doing the very thing he is claiming to be impossible.[64]

When Sextus "gives reasons" against some position, which then results in his claim that both sides are equipollent, Sextus's reasons must be claims to truth in order for them to "have weight" against the other position. If they were only impressions, then there could be no conflict; there is no conflict between (1) X seems Y to Z at T, and (2) It is not the case that X seems Y to R at T; there is a conflict between (3) X is Y, and (4) It is not the case that X is Y.[65]

Michael Frede argues that there are two different kinds of assent for the Skeptic.[66] One kind would involve the Skeptic in a self-contradiction, but the other would not. While the former involves making a claim, taking a position, and subjecting "oneself to certain canons,"[67] the latter does not; it simply involves "having a view—[and] to just have a view is to find oneself having an impression . . . but however carefully one has considered the matter it does not follow that the impression one is left with is true, nor that one thinks that it is true."[68]

On the face of it, Frede's statement seems to conflict with Sextus's characterization of impression because his statement suggests that the impression one has when one is "having a view" has a truth value; otherwise it would be unjustified for him to claim that from one's having a view, "it does not follow that the impression one is left with is true, nor that one thinks that it is true" (suggesting that either the impression may be false or that one can have a view without necessarily thinking the impression true or false). But for Sextus, impressions are neither true nor false, although they can represent or misrepresent what is true (real). I am sure that this is the sense in which Frede refers to impressions as having truth values, and this is consistent with Sextus's characterization.

The Skeptic, therefore, in considering the dogmatic claims of the Stoics (e.g., about the criterion of truth), also considers the negations of these claims (the argument and conclusion against the criterion of truth) but assents to neither in a dogmatic way. Rather, he or she finds them equiprobable (equipollent) and suspends judgment about which one to accept or reject. Frede would have us believe that this maneuver avoids the Stoic charge of pragmatic self-refutation, as Sextus also maintains.[69] If Sextus's argument and conclusion only look like assertions, but are really nonassertions (having views) about statements that appear to contradict Stoic assertions, then Sextus seems to avoid self-refutation. Furthermore, if we make a distinction between a proposition and the act of asserting a proposition (something that the Stoics did not do),[70] then one might say that while Sextus never asserts a proposition (saving himself from pragmatic self-refutation), a sentence has been nonassertively uttered that "expresses" a proposition that opposes the proposition asserted by the Stoic.[71] That is to say, the propositions differ with respect to whether the utterer assents to it or not (this saves Sextus's nonassertion from the charge that his expressed but unasserted conclusion does not contradict the conclusion of the Stoic because it is not a truth claim).[72]

As W. Kneale and M. Kneale explain, "It is the *axioma* which, for the Stoics, is primarily true or false, but the *axioma*, as we have seen, is the proposition **as asserted** rather than the proposition itself."[73] Since Sextus never asserts anything, he expresses a proposition by uttering a sentence without asserting it (i.e., assenting to it), yet the *content* of his expression opposes the *content* of the Stoic's assertion. In the language of the Stoics, Sextus has expressed a rational impression (which has propositional content) by uttering a sentence, but he has not assented to it.

If we understand Sextus's argument and conclusion as "having a view," then the charges of self-refutation are not even applicable because "having a view" relies on a notion of assertion or belief that has no connection with truth. And pragmatic self-refutation, by its very definition, presupposes that the assertions are dogmatic in that they make a claim to truth; that which is self-refuting must be a truth claim, otherwise it could not falsify itself.

In recent years, the debate between Burnyeat and Frede has been joined by others, many of whom are in support of a view like Frede's and against Burnyeat's.[74] If Burnyeat's opponents are correct and there are two different kinds of assent, this undogmatic asserting (i.e., nonasserting, having a view) can play the role that Sextus needs it to play in his argument against the criterion.

Through the argument that Sextus offers, he comes to the impression (undogmatic) that the claims appear equipollent, and thus settlement is not possible. In a different paper, Burnyeat argues, "But this appearance, so called, being the effect of argument, is only to be made sense of in terms of reason, belief and truth."[75] Here Burnyeat is arguing about the impression of equipollence, not about the argument or the conclusion of Sextus's argument against the criterion of truth (which produces the impression of equipollence).

The question of whether Sextus's Skepticism as a way of life is incoherent is tangential to our concerns, but Burnyeat's claim raises an interesting question. It seems that one could simply have an impression that two claims (contradictory conclusions) appear equipollent. The impression need not be a claim to truth *to make sense*. However, if this equipollence claim is only an impression—the impression that there is as much reason for as against ("No more this than that," as Sextus says)—then such an impression cannot itself be self-refuting. Sextus avoids the charge of self-refutation in his presentation of the argument against the criterion of truth by explaining that he never dogmatically asserts anything. To be consistent, he cannot now claim that his impression of equipollence "cancels itself along with the rest."[76] And yet, this is exactly what Sextus does say:

> [M]ost important of all, in his [the Skeptic's] enunciation of these formulae [No more this than that] he states what appears to himself and announces his own impression in an undogmatic way without making any positive assertion regarding the external realities.[77]

It seems that Sextus cannot have it both ways. Either he avoids charges of self-refutation by explaining his utterances as nonassertions (this seems to make it impossible for him to consistently claim that "No more this than that" cancels itself out), or he claims to be making assertions, and his assertions in the argument on the criterion are self-refuting, as well as his "formulae."[78] Since Sextus is very explicit in many places throughout the *Outlines* that he is not making any assertion when he states, "No more this than that," we must opt for the former interpretation of equipollence. As Sextus states:

> Then as to the formula "Nowise more" [No more this than that], even though it exhibits the character of a form of assent or of denial, we do not employ it in this way, but we take it in a loose and inexact sense, either in place of a question or in place of the phrase "I know not to which of these things I ought to assent, and to which I ought not." For our aim is to indicate what appears to us; while

as to the expression by which we indicate this we are indifferent. This point, too, should be noticed—that we utter the expression "Nowise more" not as positively affirming that it really is true and certain, but as stating in regard to it also what appears to us.[79]

If this equipollence claim is not a claim to truth, then although it is not incoherent for Sextus to utter such a claim, it is not self-refuting. This may be a problem for Sextus's Skepticism as a whole (as a way of life),[80] but his argument against the criterion of truth has not been shown to be pragmatically self-refuting.

The Argument

In the light of this analysis, let us now evaluate Sextus's argument against the criterion of truth. I will reproduce the argument and interject comments to clarify each premise; my comments will appear in brackets.

1. [SHOW] Disagreement between those who judge the truth of impressions differently is incapable of settlement. [Actually this is not a demonstration in the Stoic sense for Sextus because he makes no dogmatic assertions; he is explaining how things appear to him—that settlement *appears* impossible.]
2. A person who judges one impression true and another false does so either critically and with a proof or uncritically and without proof. [The judgment, for example, "this is white," is made either critically, that is, based on irrefutable proof, or uncritically, that is, is refutable, or alterable by reason.]
3. But a person can judge the impression in neither way because [A person can judge the impression in neither way with the result that we arrive at a settlement.]:
   a. If a person judges uncritically and without proof, then he will be discredited. [That is, the judgment is equipollent with its contradictory because no irrefutably provable reason has given it superior strength over its contradictory. Without proof it is nothing more than a bare assertion, which can be countered with a contradictory bare assertion.]
   b. If a person judges critically, then he must do so by a criterion of truth. [That is, in order to make a reasoned judgment e.g., "This is white," we need a criterion of truth for discerning appearances from reality—what merely appears white from what really is white (what is true). This reason can be a reason that settles the dispute only if it is irrefutably provable.]
   c. The criterion of truth is either claimed to be true or false. [A true criterion is one that is always successful at discerning truth, that is, at rec-

ognizing what really is. Note that each step in the argument has to do with *claims* about the truth of impressions, not how we know the truth of impressions. This is because the argument is not concerned with what is necessary to discern truth from appearance, but rather with what is necessary to settle a dispute. More will be said on this point later.]

d. If the criterion is claimed to be false, then no settlement has been achieved, and he will be discredited. [If the criterion is claimed to be false, then it is not irrefutably provable, and thus cannot settle the dispute.]

e. If the criterion is claimed to be true, then either he has a proof of the truth of the criterion or not. [Because, again, it must be irrefutably provable to settle the dispute.]

f. If a person does not have a proof, then he is discredited. [Same explanation as a and d.]

g. If a person does have a proof of the truth of the criterion, then either he claims the proof is true or he claims it is false.

h. If a person claims it is false, then he is discredited. [Same explanation as a, d, and f.]

i. If a person claims it is true, then he judges the proof true by a criterion of truth or not. [Same explanation as b.]

j. If not then he is discredited. [Same explanation as a, d, f, and h.]

k. If a person has judged it by a criterion, then either he claims the criterion true or false. [Same explanation as c.]

l. Both criterion and proof are involved in an unending or circular process of reasoning. [Either the criterion of i is the same criterion as that of b, in which case we would be using the very criterion of truth that we are critically judging, which makes the reasoning circular, or the criterion in i is different, in which case we have an infinite regress. Since either horn of the dilemma involves an impossibility, statement 3 is thereby established. And by statements 2 and 3, statement 1 is established.]

Evaluation

One interesting feature of Sextus's argument is that it is not designed to show that the Stoic is mistaken about cognitive impressions (and their truth-guaranteeing property of being evident); this latter point is argued elsewhere.[81] The "wheel" argument, as presented by Sextus, involves settling a dispute between those who disagree in their judgments about what is. The wheel argument does not claim that it is impossible to distinguish true impressions from false ones; for all we know by this argument, it may be possible. The argument is only intended to leave one with the *impression* that a dispute over differing claims cannot be settled within the constraints of Stoic epistemology.

How successful is Sextus's argument? It seems that he might be able to avoid the Stoic charge (and Burnyeat's) of self-refutation if our interpretation is correct. However, if this first difficulty is avoided, another is thereby embraced. If we interpret his formula "No more this than that" as merely an impression, not as an assertion with a truth value, and Sextus seems insistent that we do, then it appears that his overall skeptical "position" may be undermined. This is because (1) the *impression* "No more this than that" cannot possibly "cancel itself out,"[82] and (2) Sextus, then, cannot make his point that reason confounds itself, because this claim presupposes that his formula "No more this than that" cancels itself out.[83] These are problems that do not affect the validity of the wheel argument, nor do they show that his argument is somehow inconsistent or pragmatically self-refuting.

What of the argument itself? It shows that a dispute about the truth or falsity of some impression (i.e., about whether the underlying object is in fact as it appears in the impression) cannot be irrefutably proven either way. As we noted earlier, we can interpret this to mean that neither side can give a validating proof for its claim. But this is also true of deductive reasoning itself. We cannot irrefutably prove the canons of deductive logic, yet we use them to prove many things.[84] The idea of showing anything to be irrefutably provable seems to be so stringent a condition as to have little value or importance to us. Why should we have higher standards for settling a dispute than we have for accepting the canons of deductive logic? This, of course, is a question for the Stoics, not Sextus.

Indeed, if Sextus's argument is successful, it may say more against the Stoics and their stringent condition for what counts as knowledge than it does for Sextus's demonstration that using this epistemic standard as a standard for settling a dispute results in an inability to settle it. His argument calls into question whether any claim can meet the Stoic's standard. Furthermore, it only shows that, given the Stoic standard for settling a dispute, a dispute between those who claim certain impressions true and those who disagree seems impossible to settle. It shows nothing about the possibility or impossibility of knowledge or about the conditions necessary for knowledge.

This is not to say that Sextus would argue against any other position with less success. But the wheel argument, as presented by Sextus, has a very narrow focus and scope, set as it is in the context of Stoic epistemology and assumptions. In a different context, Sextus's argument may not apply. He might have to present a different argument, but his Socratic methodology would remain the same.

Since we can now understand Sextus as one who held no position, arguments we might put forward criticizing one or more of the premises in his argument would not be a criticism of Sextus's position (because he had no position), but of the Stoic's position. Thus, if I were to question the premise that a criterion is always necessary to make a judgment about an impression, or the premise that the criterion must be irrefutably provable, or the supposition that epistemic priority is necessary for the possibility of knowledge, these would not be criticisms of Sextus, but of the Stoics. These questions may be pertinent to different versions of the wheel argument presented by other philosophers, but they are best left until we deal with such versions.

In summary, then, we can draw the following conclusions:

1. Even if Sextus's argument is successful, the Stoics seem to impose unreasonably high standards for settling a dispute.

2. The lack of an ability to settle a dispute does not imply that knowledge is impossible on that subject matter, nor that disputes are impossible to settle. I could know, for instance, X is F, and someone could dispute this claim, and our dispute may be impossible to settle given these high standards for settling disputes, but this does not imply that I do not know that X is F.

3. Sextus's overall Skepticism may be in trouble. His formula "No more this than that" does not seem to be self-refuting, as he claims, and, hence, it is difficult to see how reason, then, confounds itself. This issue, however, does not affect the wheel argument.

4. If Sextus really holds *no position*, then it is difficult to see how his nonassertions could have any philosophical significance. Holding no position prevents him, in my view, from entering the philosophical arena and insulates his claims from the fires of the dialectical crucible.

We will see that many philosophers since the time of Sextus have misinterpreted him and his wheel argument. Nonetheless, their arguments may be of greater importance to our inquiry precisely for that reason. They may have wider application. Let us, then, proceed to the next major philosopher to offer a characterization of the problem of the criterion—Michael de Montaigne.

MICHAEL DE MONTAIGNE

Let us begin with Montaigne's characterization of the problem of the criterion:

> To judge of the impressions that we receive of objects, we ought to have [should have][85] a judicatory instrument; To prove the reliability of this instrument we

must have a demonstration; to prove the demonstration, an instrument: so here we are, going in a circle! Seeing that the senses cannot settle our dispute, being themselves full of uncertainty, it must be reason that is to do it; but no reason can be established without the support of another reason: so here we are running backwards to infinity![86]

This sounds quite similar to Sextus's account of the problem at PH 1.20 in that Montaigne, too, speaks in terms of settling a dispute. It seems that this similarity is more than chance. At least one account of Montaigne's *Essays* suggests that he plagiarized from Sextus:

> The unacknowledged plagiarisms in the *Essais* are far in excess of their admitted borrowing . . . to take one instance; he often cites Sextos Empirikos, though generally without naming him. Indeed, I regard Montaigne as having first introduced the great legislator of Greek skepticism into the French language. . . . At any rate all the more important of Sextos' arguments may be found in the *Essais*, and not unfrequently whole portions of the *Hypotyposes* [*Outlines*] are discovered to have been transferred bodily into its pages.[87]

Thus, it is certainly clear that Montaigne read Sextus. He even carved slogans from Sextus such as "No more this than that" into the overhead beams of his study.[88]

It should be noted that in the sixteenth century, it was common practice to "borrow" from the works of others without always citing them explicitly. There was no intention of deception, however; the audience for such writings was very well educated and the source of such "borrowed" passages was common knowledge among them. Thus, it seems that those who fault Montaigne for such practice are using a nineteenth- or twentieth-century standard to make such judgments.

Is Montaigne's understanding of the problem of the criterion any different from that of Sextus? Even though Montaigne was the reviver of Pyrrhonian Skepticism in the sixteenth century and followed Sextus closely, he may have thought that the wheel argument showed something different from what Sextus takes it to show, for example, Montaigne may have thought that knowledge was impossible. In order to determine this, I will first present a brief background of the intellectual context within which the *Essays* were written, and then extend the passage already cited, which elaborates on his argument.

Background

The wheel argument is presented in his longest essay, "The Apology for Raymond Sebond." Sebond was a fifteenth-century Spanish theologian who wrote a work entitled *Theologica Naturalis*. In this work, Sebond attempts:

to prove the truths of the Christian religion by the evidence of nature, which . . . is not only prior to, but is simpler, stronger, and more trustworthy than the evidence of the Bible and the arguments of Theology.[89]

He maintained that the evidence of nature reveals itself to us and through natural reason all truths of Christianity can be proven. This, of course, was a very unorthodox and rather audacious vindication of Christian theology, and not unsurprisingly brought Sebond censure from church authorities.

Upon the request of Montaigne's father, Montaigne translated Sebond's work into French. His "Apology" is a defense, of sorts, of Sebond's work.[90] There had been basically two objections to Sebond's work: (1) that the tenets of Christianity are matters of faith, not reason, and (2) that Sebond's arguments were poor. In the "Apology," Montaigne sets out to respond to both objections. Part of his essay is devoted to endorsing a view of Christianity that is founded entirely on faith; another part is devoted to an exposition of a Pyrrhonian-like Skepticism, which was intended to show that reason confounds itself (as Sextus had argued) and is, therefore, always unsound. He concludes that Sebond should not be criticized for having poor arguments because all reasoning is unsound. Thus, no one else has an argument that is any "better" than Sebond's.[91]

Interpretation

With this background in mind, let us turn to the passage immediately following the wheel argument:

> Our conceptions do not attach themselves to external objects, but are formed by the mediation of the senses; and the senses do not take in the external objects, but only their own impressions; and so the conception and the appearance are not of the object, but only of the impression received by the senses, which impression is a different thing from the object: therefore whoever judges by appearances judges by something other than the object.[92]

This account of "appearances" is in complete agreement with Sextus's account of impressions.

Are there differences between Sextus's account of the problem and Montaigne's? Montaigne seems to take the wheel argument to show that the senses cannot settle the dispute between those who disagree about the truth of some impressions. He states, "Seeing the senses cannot settle the dispute, being themselves full of uncertainty. . . ."[93] Yet the argument he offers establishes no such conclusion. The argument, if sound, establishes that if settlement of the dispute involves establishing or proving one side with certainty, then the dispute cannot be settled. *The senses* do not settle the dispute. A criterion established with certainty by an established proof settles the dispute. Montaigne's apparent confusion may simply be due to his rambling style in the essay and may not indicate a break with Sextus. Montaigne's standard for settling the dispute seems to be certainty, which is somewhat different from Sextus's irrefutable provability. Irrefutable provability seems to be a more stringent and narrow standard than certainty, for while the former guarantees the latter, the latter may be achieved in other ways (perhaps by intuition).

The upshot of the passage above is that if the senses were a source of certainty, then they would settle the dispute. Sextus would probably not disagree with this. Thus, while there may be small differences in their respective accounts, the spirit of Montaigne's argument seems the same as Sextus's. It seems that the intent of Montaigne's remark about the senses is that irrefutable provability is the only way for us to achieve such certainty; otherwise, the wheel argument would make no sense in this context. Nonetheless, I am left with the impression that Montaigne takes the argument to show that we cannot achieve knowledge through the senses, because they are full of uncertainty. This is not endorsed by Sextus, and at many places in the essay, Montaigne states that the account he is describing is undogmatic—takes no position—exactly the way Sextus argues. There is an explanation for this "trace of dogmatism" in Montaigne's argument, and I will offer it shortly.

There is one difference between Montaigne and Sextus that may be important. Sextus holds no position whatsoever, on any matter, while it seems that Montaigne must hold a position in order to be a good Christian. There is at least an apparent conflict between his complete endorsement and avowal of the truth of Christianity and his arguments in favor of complete Skepticism. It has been suggested that just as Sextus accepted custom in his practical guide to life,[94] so too, Montaigne is simply accepting custom and tradition in accepting Christianity. But even if this interpretation is convincing, it does not circumvent the problem; Montaigne maintained a position concerning Christianity's *truth and knowability*. If this is correct, then an irrefutably provable criterion is not the only road to certainty; God may bestow it on us in a vision or intuition.

This makes Montaigne's account of the problem somewhat different from Sextus's account. Montaigne leaves open an alternative, which Sextus would not allow—knowledge through divine revelation or intuition. This may explain why Montaigne's account of the wheel argument seems to me to be more like an argument against the possibility of knowledge through our sense impressions than an argument against the possibility of settling the dispute between those who disagree about impressions. Indeed, Popkin seems to interpret it that way, when he says, "The critique of sense knowledge leads to the crescendo of this symphony of doubt, the problem of the criterion."[95]

This explains my suspicions about Montaigne's wheel argument (i.e., that it is intended to show that we cannot achieve knowledge through the senses because they are full of uncertainty), because Montaigne's position as a Christian thinker—his affirmation of the truth and knowability of Christianity, and his contention that *only* through faith and the grace of God *could* we achieve such knowledge[96]—is compatible with this only if we think of the wheel argument as a polemic against the possibility of certainty and knowledge through the senses and reason. This is further supported by the following:

> If our sensible and intellectual faculties are without foundation and without footing ... it seems vain that we suffer our judgment to be carried away by any part of their operation, whatever the appearance that it seems to put before us. ... Either we can judge absolutely or we absolutely cannot.[97]

If he really meant, as Sextus did, simply to present arguments in response to someone else's argument or claim to knowledge, then we would expect him to argue that there is as much reason to reject Christianity as there is to accept it; and so too with God's existence. Yet he states, "True and essential reason ... is lodged in the bosom of God," and further, "Now there can be no first principles for men, if they are not revealed to them by Divinity."[98] This seems to indicate that knowledge is not possible through human reasoning. This is a position. Yet knowledge and truth seem possible through "revelation" or "intuition" from God. This is also a position. So while Sextus is undogmatic tout à fait, Montaigne, while professing suspension of judgment, cannot seem to avoid endorsing the truth of Christianity. The tenets of Christianity are not "No more this than that."

This endorsement, of course, then reintroduces the problem of the criterion. Montaigne asserts the truth of Christianity; others assert the falsity of Christianity (these are Montaigne's "false sects"). In order to judge between them (and settle the dispute), we need a criterion. Montaigne claims that divine revelation is the criterion. But how do we discern what is divinely inspired and what is not? Since the dispute cannot be settled by proof, we suspend judgment. There is as much reason to believe the one as there is to believe the other. We can only speak justifiably of appearances, which lay no claim to truth. As we noted earlier, it is actually inappropriate to speak in terms of truth and falsity with respect to appearances. Truth does not apply to appearances. Therefore, if Christianity is a matter of appearances, it is not a matter of truth and falsity.

Regardless of what Montaigne claims, his position seems problematic in a way that Sextus's is not. In maintaining the truth of Christianity, he lays himself open to the problem of the criterion. The traditional response to such difficulties has been to underscore the distinction between faith and reason. In other words, in maintaining the truth of Christianity—a matter of faith only—it is no wonder we run into logical difficulties when we try to *reason* about its truth. We should expect such difficulties, not because Christianity may not be true, but because logic and reason confound themselves.

However, the very distinction made between faith and reason is also a position that Sextus would indeed question. I can see no consistent way to be a thoroughgoing Pyrrhonian Skeptic and a devout Christian. While Montaigne claims to be a Pyrrhonian Skeptic, he seems to be a closet dogmatist! If so, is the problem of the criterion, as presented by Montaigne, the *same* problem that Sextus presented? Both ask the question: How can we settle the dispute between those who claim an impression true or false, and those who disagree? But to pose the same problem, they must also make all the same presuppositions in asking the question. And it seems likely that their presuppositions differ in some important respects. In so far as their presuppositions differ, their characterizations of the problem of the criterion are characterizations of different problems.[99] Both characterizations of the problem should be clearly distinguished from the following problems: How is knowledge possible through the senses? Is knowledge possible through the senses or reason? Is knowledge possible? These problems would all be misinterpretations of Sextus's and Montaigne's characterization of the problem of the criterion. It is Montaigne's background assumptions and presuppositions that distinguish him from Sextus Empiricus and present unique problems for his philosophy as a whole.

CARDINAL D. J. MERCIER

Cardinal Mercier is credited by Chisholm with reviving the ancient problem of the criterion for the twentieth century. It seems that the problem lay dormant for quite some time after Montaigne's essay. Mercier cites Montaigne's characterization of the problem from "The Apology for Raymond Sebond" for his characterization of the problem:

> To form a judgment on the appearances we receive of things we must have what will serve as a standard of judgment; to verify this standard we must have a proof; to verify this proof we must have a standard: and so we have a real spinning wheel. Then again our senses alone will not put an end to the difficulty,

reason must be brought in; but any argument from reason will not stand without another argument to establish it: and so we go on forever.[100]

He notes, however, that by this argument we "are forced to conclude that there is no certain truth and that universal doubt is the law of mind."[101] This conclusion seems to be in sharp contrast with Sextus's suspension of judgment and Montaigne's espousal of suspension of judgment. With the very same argument as Montaigne, Mercier concludes something quite different. His own wording of the problem, which is supplied as a supplement to his quote of Montaigne, states:

> Before we can affirm a proposition as certain we must, unless we are willing to admit it on mere *a priori* grounds, verify it by means of some other judgment which shall serve as a criterion of truth. Yet this criterion itself must be in its own turn verified, and this can only be done by means of some other criterion, and so on *ad infinitum*. Thus do we argue in a circle, and are forced to conclude that there is no certain truth and that universal doubt is the law of our mind.[102]

Mercier does not mean to say that before we can *simply affirm* a proposition as certain we must verify it by a criterion of truth that is also verified, and so on Simply to affirm a proposition as certain, we need only assert it as certain. Mercier must mean something different. A clue to his meaning is found in the following:

> It is a fact . . . that we are in possession of a number of propositions of which we think, rightly or wrongly, that we are certain, propositions to which we give a spontaneous and even irresistible assent; spontaneous certitude does exist as a subjective fact. The question to be determined is whether this spontaneous assent is *justifiable*; whether by deliberate reflection upon a proposition to which we spontaneously assent we can *show* this spontaneous assent to be legitimate, thus obtaining reflex assent and *true certitude*.[103]

And further:

> The claim of the real skeptic is that we must regard as doubtful not only each of the acts of the human reason but also its very capability of arriving at a knowledge of the truth; and further that it is impossible to find a way out of this doubt.[104]

While the idea of "certain" does not carry with it the idea of irrefutable provability (as it did for the Stoics and Sextus), it does involve *justification*; an objective legitimation through some kind of demonstrative showing. Presumably, however, such a showing would, by definition, prove irrefutably that the proposition in question was true. So, we can understand "affirm a proposition as certain" to mean "affirm with a justification a proposition as certain." And if this is what Mercier means, then it does not follow from the fact that a person cannot affirm with a justification as certain, for example, X is P, that X is P is not certain for that person. One might *be* certain or *be* justified in affirming a proposition as certain without being able to affirm *with* a justification a proposition as certain. Thus, it seems as if Mercier has erred in his conclusion to the wheel argument. He has misinterpreted the original wheel argument. And even concerning the Skeptic's claim to suspend judgment, Mercier mistakenly construes this as a *principle*: "The skeptic then has no right to *lay down as a principle* that it is doubtful whether the mind is capable of knowing."[105]

Mercier then proceeds to argue (unlike Sextus and Montaigne) that the wheel argument (he calls it the argument drawn from the vicious circle) is mistaken, and that the mind is capable of knowing truth. Mercier will show the "error" of the wheel argument and also offer a "solution" to this problem. Before considering his argument against the wheel argument, however, we should examine what conditions Mercier thinks any satisfactory solution to the problem must meet. Mercier has offered three such conditions:

> If there is any knowledge which bears the mark of truth, if the intellect does have a way of distinguishing the true and the false, in short, *if* there *is* a criterion of truth, then this criterion should satisfy three conditions: it should be *internal*, *objective* and *immediate*.[106]

This is a metacriterion for possible criteria of truth. There is an important question to address at this point: How satisfactory is this metacriterion? The quotation from Mercier simply ends with the questions: "Is there a criterion of truth that satisfies these conditions? If so, what is it?"[107] Mercier offers reasons for accepting his three conditions:

> It should be *internal*. No reason or rule of truth that is provided by an *external authority* can serve as an ultimate criterion. For the reflective doubts that are essential to criteriology can and should be applied to this authority itself. The mind cannot attain to certainty until it has found *within itself* a sufficient reason for adhering to the testimony of such an authority.
>
> The criterion should be *objective*. The ultimate reason for believing cannot be a merely *subjective* state of the thinking subject. A man is aware that he can reflect upon his psychological states in order to control them. Knowing that he has this ability, he does not, so long as he has not made use of it, have the right to be sure. The ultimate ground of certitude cannot consist in a subjective feel-

ing. It can be found only in that which, objectively, produces this feeling and is adequate to reason.

Finally, the criterion must be *immediate*. To be sure, a certain conviction may rest upon many different reasons some of which are subordinate to others. But if we are to avoid an infinite regress, then we must find a ground of assent that presupposes no other. We must find an *immediate* criterion of certitude.[108]

I have two objections to this position.

1. Mercier's reasons for these three conditions are unconvincing. For example, consider the first condition: internal or intrinsic. Basically, Mercier attempts to refute some of the traditional arguments given by philosophers with opposing views, and then offers a few statements intended to convince the reader of the necessity of his view. After presenting arguments against de Boland, Lamennais, and Rousseau, he concludes:

> The traditionalists attempted to find the guarantee of certitude outside our intelligence, in other words an *extrinsic criterion*. But if my intellect can attain to the truth, it is within myself that I must find its guarantee. The criterion must be *intrinsic*.[109]

From both of the references above, it seems that his argument comes to this: our criterion of truth cannot be external because (1) reflective doubts are essential to Criteriology, (2) these doubts should be applied to this external authority, and (3) only an internal authority found by the mind within itself can be sufficient for adhering to the testimony of such an authority.

But what is it about an external authority that makes it, apparently in principle, never sufficient for adhering to its testimony? What is it about an internal authority that makes it superior? Might not the mind dupe itself?[110] Might not an external authority be better than an internal one for this very reason? There is certainly much room for debate here. How can our criterion be *both* internal *and* objective? If it is internal, one might argue, it must be subjective.[111] It seems quite conceivable that we could make a strong case for conditions of external, subjective, and mediate, or some mix of the two trios, or a fourth or fifth condition as well. Perhaps consistency is a good candidate. How would we decide such disputes? What reason do we have to think that Mercier's metacriterion has some privileged status? My point is simply that his arguments do not provide us with such acceptable reasons.

2. Most importantly, Mercier's metacriterion seems subject to the very problem that it is intended to resolve. In other words, how do we know that this metacriterion is a good metacriterion for picking out good criteria of truth? In order to know that my metacriterion succeeds, it seems that I must

already know how to determine what are good and bad criteria of truth. Thus, we are back on the wheel again. We now have the problem of the metacriterion. Mercier's conditions do not show how to avoid this. We have good reason to question Mercier's metacriterion as a means of solving the problem of the criterion.

Let us now examine why he rejects the wheel argument as false and what his "solution" is to the problem. Mercier argues that "the argument he draws from the vicious circle wrongly supposes that we must always justify a proposition by means of a criterion distinct from the proposition itself."[112]

His main thesis is then:

> *When we form immediate judgments of the truth of which we are certain, we as a matter of fact attribute the predicate to the subject precisely on account of the objective identity manifested between the predicate and the subject, and not because this union is demanded exclusively by the natural constitution of our mind.*—The only possible proof of this thesis is the testimony of the fact itself as witnessed *by our consciousness.*[113]

Mercier uses the example of the judgment that the three angles of a triangle are equal to two right angles. He maintains that the "necessary and sufficient condition for the exclusion of my doubt and for the possession of certitude is the perception I have of the objective identity of the subject and the predicate of my judgment."[114] It should be noted here that Mercier believes that his solution to the problem (at least at this point) involves what he calls the possibility of knowledge in "the ideal order"; in other words, he wants to consider first whether knowledge concerning relations is possible, and then examine the question of whether those relations are exemplified in the real world. This explains his use of a "part-whole" example and the triangle example cited.

Technically, according to those who first posed the problem, if we are not making a judgment about what *is*, then we are not making a judgment; and thus, whatever we are doing, it has no truth value. So, the content of the problem seems to have changed with Mercier's interpretation. Mercier actually thinks that the dispute between those who claim an impression true and those who claim it false is a different problem.[115] He does, however, believe that by establishing knowledge in the ideal order he can then also establish knowledge in the "real order," that is, about what *is*. These arguments need not concern us here, for they are not essential for our treatment of Mercier.

For our purposes, since Sextus called everything into question, we will ignore Mercier's distinction and evaluate his argument notwithstanding his departure from Sextus; indeed, Mercier intends judgments of the ideal order to have truth values.

The most obvious problem for Mercier's "solution" is that it is not a solution to the problem stated. Even if Mercier were correct about "objective identity," and such, his solution is not one that can objectively settle a dispute; it cannot objectively justify one's affirmation of certitude about some proposition. It merely claims to afford us with the necessary and sufficient conditions for the *possession* of certitude, not for its *justification*. Satisfying his condition does not, as Mercier says, "*show* this spontaneous assent to be legitimate,"[116] at least not to anyone who is looking for some kind of a demonstrative showing, or who questions Mercier's claim concerning certitude. *My* perception may be sufficient to exclude *my* doubt, but I see no reason to think that my perception is sufficient to exclude the Skeptic's doubt. And only this will settle the dispute. Thus, not only has Mercier not solved the problem stated, he has also changed the problem, then failed to solve the changed problem.

One might think that even though Mercier cites Montaigne, who speaks about "adjudication" ("settling the dispute" in Sextus's terms), Mercier thinks that the problem of the criterion is not a problem about adjudication or settling a dispute, but rather about the necessary and sufficient conditions for the *possession of certitude*. Although he may not have solved Sextus's problem, perhaps he has solved his own. Furthermore, even if Mercier did not mean something different from Sextus when he spoke of the problem of the criterion, and even if this interpretation is not an accurate *historical* analysis of Mercier's position (which I maintain), perhaps it is worth considering from a purely philosophical point of view. Perhaps the problem Mercier attempts to solve is: What are the necessary and sufficient conditions of certitude?

One might reasonably argue that there is rational doubt about the correct answer to the question posed. In order for Mercier to solve this problem, his answer must remove rational doubt about the correct answer to the question. I have two responses to this consideration:

1. Let us assume that Mercier is correct in asserting that the "necessary and sufficient condition for the exclusion of my doubt and for the possession of certitude is the perception I have of the objective identity of the subject and the predicate of my judgment."[117] Mercier states that he needs to "*show* this spontaneous assent to be legitimate, thus obtaining reflex assent and true certitude."[118] It seems that the only kind of "showing" required to satisfy Mercier's necessary and sufficient condition is a "showing to oneself," which is, by current usage, a peculiar way to show anything in order to legitimate it. Nonetheless, we could interpret "showing" to mean "showing to one-

self," in which case meeting Mercier's condition would be *that* kind of a showing, and a kind of "legitimating to oneself."

2. Mercier claims that one possesses certitude when and only when one perceives the "objective identity" of the subject and the predicate of one's judgment. He offers the example of the judgment that the three angles of a triangle are equal to two right angles. One possesses certitude when and only when one perceives the objective identity of the subject—the three angles of the triangle—and the predicate—two right angles. Now suppose that I make the following judgment: "I feel pain" (or "I seem to see yellow" or "I am thinking of a tropical island"). It seems clear that since I perceive no objective identity of the subject and the predicate of my judgment, I *could* not be certain about any first person, present tense, mental report on Mercier's account. Yet Mercier offers no reason why such judgments *could* not be certain. It seems that there might be many ways to possess certitude.

Therefore, without going into an analysis of Mercier's concept of "objective identity" and his entire epistemology (which would be tangential to our focus of concern), we can conclude that, at best, Mercier has provided *a* sufficient condition for the possession of certitude. If we begin to raise questions about how one can ever be sure that one is really perceiving an "objective identity" and not merely fooling oneself, then the problem of providing some kind of "objective legitimation" or demonstrative showing arises again. It seems clear to me, however, from the passages cited, that Mercier was looking for a way to *show*, not merely to himself, but to others, how knowledge and certainty are possible.

It is worth noting that P. Coffey, a pupil of Mercier, who is also credited with aiding in the revival of the problem of the criterion, supports Mercier's position that the criterion for some judgments is its own justification. But he adds:

> [O]f course, if we fail to convince the skeptic that any of the judgments to which he admits he is forced to assent by psychological necessity, reveal on analysis a character which is at once a criterion or index of their real objectivity and truth, and at the same time a justification of that criterion, then we must leave him in his skepticism.[119]

Thus, he seems to realize that Mercier's argument does not irrefutably prove anything or settle a dispute, for the Skeptic may not be convinced. Apparently, this is acceptable to him. But Coffey misses the whole point of the ancient wheel argument with such acceptance. The dispute has not been settled. Claiming to possess certitude, or even possessing certitude, is not the issue. We need an objective justification to settle the issue. And my perception does not establish any objective justification, even if we are speaking of judgments in the "ideal realm." Remember that even necessary truths are impressions for Sextus—all concepts being derived through impressions—and are subject to the force of the wheel argument.

Mercier, then, has not succeeded in solving the problem of the necessary and sufficient conditions for the possession of certitude. It is also clear that his characterization of the problem of the criterion is quite different from Sextus and Montaigne, because Mercier makes different presuppositions when citing the question posed by Montaigne.[120] Indeed, he may have done more to confuse the issues than to clarify them. In the next chapters, we will look to two contemporary sources for their analyses of the problem of the criterion.

NOTES

1. All references to the writings of Sextus Empiricus refer to R. G. Bury's edition of the Greek text, *Sextus Empiricus*, tr. and ed. by R. G. Bury, 4 vols. (Cambridge: Harvard University Press, 1933–49). I follow convention by abbreviating with "PH" for *Outlines of Pyrrhonism* and "M" for *Adversus Mathematicos*, which includes both *Against The Professors* and *Against The Dogmatists*. The first number following the abbreviation is the book number, and the second identifies the line numbers on the English translation side of the Bury edition.

2. PH 2.19–20.

3. PH 1.114–17.

4. Myles Burnyeat has an excellent discussion of the importance of this dialectical context in understanding Sextus's arguments, in "Protagoras and Self-Refutation in Later Greek Philosophy," *Philosophical Review* 85 (Jan. 1976): 44–69. Mark L. McPherran offers other insights about the importance of the dialectical nature of Sextus's overall project in "Skeptical Homeopathy and Self-refutation," *Phronesis* 32 (1987): 290–328.

5. See Plato, *Apology*, in *The Collected Dialogues of Plato*, ed. Edith Hamilton (Princeton, N. J.: Princeton University Press, 1961), 21a–e, 3–27. Although Socrates never stopped searching, he never attained his goal.

6. See Burnyeat, "Protagoras and Self-Refutation," 44–69.

7. Michael Frede, "Stoics and Skeptics on Clear and Distinct Impressions," in *The Skeptical Tradition*, ed. Myles Burnyeat (Berkeley: University of California Press, 1983), 65–93. This essay also appears in M. Frede, *Essays in Ancient Philosophy* (Minneapolis: University of Minnesota Press, 1987), 151–76.

8. Frede, Ibid.

9. For a more detailed explanation, see B. Mates, Stoic Logic (Berkeley: University of California Press, 1973); A. A. Long, *Hellenistic Philosophy* (London: G. Duckworth, 1974); and Burnyeat, "Protagoras and Self-Refutation," 44–69.

10. Frede, "Stoics and Skeptics," 69.
11. Sextus, M 1.402. See also M 1.248, 252, and Cicero, *Academica,* ed. J. S. Reid (London: Macmillan, 1885), ii, 18.
12. Long, *Hellenistic Philosophy,* 127.
13. Ibid. Long cites *Stoicorum Veterum Fragmenta (Fragments of the Early Stoics),* ed. H. von Arnim (Leipzig: Teubner, 1903–24, reprinted Stuttgart: Teubner, 1964), vol. ii, frag. 54.
14. For an excellent discussion of this point, see Frede, "Stoics and Skeptics," 69.
15. See Frede, "Stoics and Skeptics," 72–76, for a more complete discussion of this point. Also Mates, chap. 2; McPherran, "Skeptical Homeopathy," 296 fn; and Charlotte L. Stough, *Greek Skepticism* (Berkeley and Los Angeles: University of California Press, 1969), chap. 3, 36–37 fn.
16. Frede, "Stoics and Skeptics," 76.
17. See Stough, *Greek Skepticism,* chap. 3. Her term for cognitive impressions is "cataleptic impression," after the Greek "καταληπτικη."
18. Sextus, M 1.253–54. For an interesting argument that opposes the claim that the Stoics changed their position, and on the notion of a cognitive impression, see J. M. Rist, "The Criterion of Truth," in *Stoic Philosophy* by J. M. Rist (Cambridge: Cambridge University Press, 1969), 133–51.
19. Sextus, M 1.253–57. From this passage it is unclear just what an obstacle is. Stough interprets "no obstacle" as "provided there is no reason for not accepting it," *Greek Skepticism,* 39 fn. This is consistent with the text but nonetheless presents problems for the Stoics; what counts as a "reason" for not accepting? F. H. Sandbach also discusses cognitive impressions in "Phantasia Kataleptike" in *Problems in Stoicism,* ed. A. A. Long (London: Athlone Press, 1971), 9–21; and notes the difficulties involved in clearly explaining this Stoic notion. This is a problem for Stoic epistemology and I will not dwell on it here.
20. Sextus, M 1.257.
21. For a more thorough discussion of this, see Frede, "Stoics and Skeptics."
22. Sextus, M 1.151–52.
23. Cicero offers a metaphor to explain the difference between firm and weak assent:

> And Zeno used to make this point by using a gesture. When he held out his hand with open fingers, he would say, "this is what a presentation is like." Then when he had closed his fingers a bit, he said, "assent is like this." And when he had compressed it completely and made a fist, he said that this was grasping (and on the basis of this comparison he even gave it the name *katalepsis* [grasp], which had not previously existed). But when he put his left hand over it and compressed it tightly and powerfully, he said that knowledge was this sort of thing and that no one except a wise man possessed it.

[*Academica* from *Hellenistic Philosophy,* tr. B. Inwood and L. P. Gerson (Indianapolis: Hackett, 1988), 91.]

Rist argues that "grasp" must have two different senses—one weak, which corresponds to the grasping of perception (belief), and one firm, which corresponds to the grasping of knowledge. (See "The Criterion of Truth," in *Stoic Philosophy*, 139.)

24. Long, *Hellenistic Philosophy*, 130. This seems like a misleading interpretation of "irrefutable" because it seems to preclude knowledge of anything contingent, such as "X is F," which is the very topic under discussion. [Long speaks of assenting to the impression that "there really is a black dog which we see" (p. 127).] I believe that Long means to say that "irrefutable" means that its possessor can give a validating proof of what he or she claims to know. I say this because Long likens irrefutable knowledge to Plato's "tether" in the *Meno*, that is, giving an account (λογοσ) of how one knows. Later Long states, "Unlike the ordinary man who utters some true statements which he cannot prove against every attempt to overturn them, the wise man's judgments are infallible *since he knows why each of them must be true*" (my emphasis). This is also supported by Diogenes Laertius in *Lives of Eminent Philosophers*, tr. R. D. Hicks (Cambridge: Harvard University Press, 1925), in two vols. 7.165, 7.47, hereafter referred to as DL, and in Cicero, *Academica* 2.144–45, in *Hellenistic Philosophy*, (Indianapolis: Hackett, 1988), 91.

25. In other words, (h) is irrefutable, or S can prove (h) by means of propositions that are necessarily true, or S knows a deductive validating proof of (h). These alternative ways of expressing "S's assent to (h) is firm" are supposed to be equivalent to each other, even though they appear to be quite different. This is a problem for interpreters of Stoic epistemology to sort out, and I will not dwell upon it here. I also recognize that the phrase "irrefutable provability" seems redundant; if something is provable, then it cannot be refuted. But "irrefutable provability" also indicates an unshakable, unswerving hold on that which is apprehended—one that "cannot be shaken by argument" (DL 7.47).

26. Sextus, M 1.432–33.

27. Gregory Vlastos has a discussion of this point in "Socrates' Disavowal of Knowledge," *Philosophical Quarterly* 35, no. 138 (Jan. 1985): 1–31.

28. For a thorough, clear discussion of the differences between Pyrrhonian and Academic Skepticism see Stough's *Greek Skepticism*. Hereafter in this chapter, I will use the term "Skeptic" to mean "Pyrrhonian Skeptic" and "Academic Skeptic" for the dogmatic sort.

29. DL 7.47.

30. Frede, "Stoics and Skeptics," 88.

31. See note 28 and Charlotte Stough, "Sextus Empiricus on Non-Assertion," *Phronesis* 29 (1984): 137–64; somewhat related to this is Jonathan Barnes, "The Beliefs of a Pyrrhonist," *Proceedings of the Cambridge Philological Society* 208 (1982): 1–29.

32. Sextus explains equipollence as "equality in respect of probability and improbability, to indicate that no one of the conflicting judgments takes precedence of any other as being more probable" (PH 1.10).

33. Sextus, PH 1.8.

34. Sextus, PH 1.26.

35. See Sextus (PH 1.16), "Has the Skeptic a Doctrinal Rule?" Also see Frede,

"The Skeptic's Two Kinds of Assent and the Question of the Possibility of Knowledge," in *Essays in Ancient Philosophy*, 201–24; and the references in notes 28 and 31 above.

36. See M. Burnyeat, "Can the Skeptic Live His Skepticism?" in *Doubt and Dogmatism*, ed. M. Schonfield, M. Burnyeat and J. Barnes (Oxford: Clarendon Press, 1980), 20–53; Frede, "Two Kinds of Assent," 201–24; McPherran, "Skeptical Homeopathy," 290–328; Barnes, "Beliefs of a Pyrrhonist," 1–29; Stough, "Sextus Empiricus," 137–64; Bailey, "Pyrrhonian Skepticism and the Self-Refutation Argument," *Philosophical Quarterly* 40 (Jan. 1990): 27–44.

37. Sextus, PH 1.19–20.

38. See Burnyeat's discussion of this point in "Idealism and Greek Philosophy: What Descartes Saw and Berkeley Missed," *Philosophical Review* 91, no. 1 (Jan. 1982): 1–40. Charlotte Stough discusses Sextus's identification of impression with phenomenon, and his psychological explanation of assent to an impression in *Greek Skepticism*, 115–25. At PH 1.21–25, Sextus explains that impressions or phenomena are the Skeptic's undisputed guide to life. Impressions are the criterion used as a "standard of action" (PH 1.21).

39. Sextus, PH 1.22.

40. See Burnyeat, "Idealism and Greek Philosophy," for a more complete discussion of this point.

41. Stough's term for a nonassertion in "Sextus Empiricus."

42. Rist speaks as if even bare sensing (as he calls it) "as an animal would see" could be appropriately termed true, as all would be true—meaning merely "All sensations are in fact sensations of what they are sensations" (*Stoic Philosophy*, 135). Bare sensing involves no recognition, no mental activity on what is sensed, and no assent. This is contrasted with "perception," which does involve recognition and assent. Rist likens this distinction to Aristotle's distinction in *De Anima* between the functions of the individual senses and the "common" sense. Again, when assent is firm, we have a cognitive impression (Rist calls it "recognizable presentation").

43. Stough points out that Sextus never makes clear whether having a (sensory) impression is the mere passive sensation of being affected (say) in a whitish way or ". . . the experience (involving intellectual synthesis) of something's being white, that is, an impression that . . . 'this appears white'" ("Sextus Empiricus," 141 fn). She also questions whether Sextus's notion of impression is wholly adopted from the Stoics, because the Stoics believed in nonsensory impressions and there is some question as to whether Sextus subscribes to this as well. [See Burnyeat, "Can the Skeptic Live," 34; M. Frede, "Review of Greek Skepticism," Journal of Philosophy 70 (1973): 805–10.]

44. An interesting question that arises here concerns whether such statements, which Sextus concedes serve as guides to life, express *beliefs* that the Skeptic maintains. I will try to address this question later as it bears upon the issue of coherency in the Skeptic's attack on Stoicism and on the issue of self-refutation.

45. See Burnyeat, "Idealism and Greek Philosophy," 27, who cites Galen, *De pulsuum differentiis*, VII 711, 1–3 Kuhn, available also in Karl Deichegraber, *Die Grei-*

chische Empirikerschule (Berlin: Weidmann, 1930), frag. 75.135, 28–30. See also Frede, "Stoics and Skeptics," 87, where he states that in other contexts, the Skeptic is "quite willing to challenge the dogma of the impression as a given."

46. Arne Naess, *Skepticism* (New York: Humanities, 1968), 21.

47. Of course, that cannot be the entire explanation, because there are impressions that involve concepts and have no propositional content; perhaps, for example, John's being tall. Sextus offers no clear explanation of how impressions have propositional content and yet are not subject to truth values. Perhaps this is because, as Stough points out, "the distinction between assertion and nonassertion marks off categories of *speech* rather than kinds of things. . . . His words will be informative (of his assent) but will make no claim about what is so" ("Sextus Empiricus," 143).

48. Stough, "Sextus Empiricus," 143. At PH 1.191, Sextus also states: "Then as to the formula 'Nowise more,' even though it exhibits the character of a form of assent or of denial, we do not employ it in this way, but we take it in a loose and inexact sense, either in place of a question or in place of the phrase 'I know not to which of these things I ought to assent, and to which I ought not.' For our aim is to indicate what appears to us; while as to the expression by which we indicate this we are indifferent."

49. Sextus, M 1.151.

50. Unreasoned disagreements are of no value for they are merely unfounded claims—what Sextus calls "uncritical" judgments, which are incapable of rationally settling anything.

51. Sextus, M 1.154.

52. Sextus, PH 1.8, my emphasis.

53. Sextus, PH1.10.

54. Sextus, PH 1.202–05. Also see Burnyeat, "Protagoras and Self-Refutation," for a criticism of Bury's translation of "logos" (λογοσ) as "argument." He prefers "dogmatic assertion" and I agree.

55. See P. Hallie, *Skepticism, Man and God* (Middletown, Conn.: Wesleyan University Press, 1964), 34, n. 1, for a discussion of this point.

56. See Long, *Hellenistic Philosophy*, 92, and Frede, "Stoics and Skeptics," 85–86.

57. Sextus, M 2.480–81. Indeed, this is one of the features that distinguishes Pyrrhonian Skepticism from Academic Skepticism.

58. To be sure, other problems will then arise, but they will be different from the problem of the criterion that Sextus has presented.

59. Burnyeat, "Protagoras and Self-Refutation." Burnyeat relies on a distinction between pragmatic, absolute and operational self-refutation developed by J. L. Mackie in "Self-Refutation—A Formal Analysis," *Philosophical Quarterly* 14, no. 56 (July 1964): 193–203.

60. Burnyeat, "Protagoras and Self-Refutation," 52.

61. Ibid.

62. If the problem of the criterion relies on a dispute (see chapter 1) and the claims of one of the disputants are pragmatically self-refuting, then there is no longer a reasoned dispute.

63. See Sextus, M 7.443–44.
64. Burnyeat, "Protagoras and Self-Refutation," 53–54.
65. As Burnyeat argues: "If my arguing for a thesis is actually to falsify it, what I produce in its support has got to be real, not just intended argument or reasons. If I merely purport to prove there is no proof but do not actually do so, my procedure does not definitely establish the reality of proof; it only concedes to be true the very thing I am at the same time denying" ("Protagoras and Self-Refutation," 54).
66. Frede, "Skeptic's Two Kinds of Assent."
67. Ibid., 206.
68. Ibid.
69. Stough argues: "The Skeptic's speech, *construed as assertion*, is self-refuting. . . . Non-assertion does not prevent the Skeptic from using reason to rebut dogmatic theories. Since the dogmatist is committed to criteria of valid, true and *apodeictic* arguments (PH II.135ff., M VIII.300ff.), he must be persuaded in his own terms. If the Skeptic 'demonstrates' according to those criteria that 's is p,' his conclusion (construed as 's appears p') does not actually contradict his antagonist's *assertion* to the contrary. But if the dogmatist accepts the Skeptic's reasoning as sound, he must also accept his own thesis is refuted. For he, (unlike the Skeptic) does not eschew assertion. The Skeptic's aim in his polemic against the dogmatist always has this practical dimension" (PH III.280–81); ("Sextus Empiricus," 144, n. 12).

Stough notes that this interpretation presents difficulties for Sextus's Skepticism-as-a-way-of-life (Burnyeat's incoherency charge), but it seems to me that it also presents difficulties for explaining why the Stoic should accept his argument if it is not an assertion. I believe that the answer to this difficulty will be explained shortly; cf. notes 70, 71, 72, and 73.

70. See Burnyeat, "Protagoras and Self-Refutation," 54–55. For a more detailed discussion, see W. Kneale and M. Kneale, *The Development of Logic* (Oxford: Clarendon Press, 1962), 144–45, 153–58.

71. As Kneale and Kneale explain, the Stoics had a theory of meaning, which involved *lekta* (λεκτα)—things signified or expressed. It means literally "what is meant"; *axioma* (αξιομα) is a proposition, which is a kind of lekton—the only one that is called true or false. "Although *lekta* are to be distinguished from any spoken sounds, words, or sentences, it is clear that a *lekton* can be identified only by the use of a word or sentence *which expresses it*" (Kneale and Kneale, *Development of Logic*, 143, my emphasis). Hence, we could say that Sextus utters a sentence nonassertively, which expresses a proposition whose *content* opposes the *content* of the proposition *asserted* by the Stoic. So it is the *meanings* expressed by the utterances of the Stoic and Skeptic that oppose each other—an opposition of meaning. Sextus withholds assent to the proposition expressed by his utterance, while the Stoic assents to the proposition expressed by his utterance—thereby asserting it. This is consistent with the Stoic account of assent and how it is a voluntary action after consideration of a proposition (so is the withholding of assent). If, according to the Stoics, the proposition only has truth value if asserted, then it still has *meaning* before the act of assent; and hence, meanings can still oppose each other. One might think of it as the opposition

in meaning in the concepts (not propositions) "John's being tall" and "John's being short."

72. As Burnyeat argues concerning Sextus's claim that there is no such thing as reason, evidence, and proof: "There are indeed only two possibilities: either he declines to debate the question and cannot claim the edge over an opponent who rejects the thesis, or he does not but is willing to argue his case—that is, give reason, evidence, or proof for it—and promptly finds himself going over to the other man's view. Either way he loses. His thesis is necessarily a loser" (Burnyeat, "Protagoras and Self-Refutation," 55).

73. Kneale and Kneale, *Development of Logic*, 153; the boldface is my emphasis. Hence, the reason the Stoic must accept the Skeptic's reasons as ones that contradict his or her own, is because the contents do oppose one another and the only difference between the two (that one is an assertion and one is not) is not one that the Stoic can discern; furthermore, assertion is the language of the Stoic. The fact that the contents of the two claims oppose one another saves Sextus from the charge of insincerity and from Burnyeat's criticism.

74. See Gisela Striker, "Skeptical Strategies," in *Doubt and Dogmatism*, 54–83; Stough, "Sextus Empiricus"; Barnes, "Beliefs of a Pyrrhonist"; McPherran, "Skeptical Homeopathy"; Michael Williams, "Skepticism Without Theory," *Review of Metaphysics* 41 (March 1988): 547–88; Bailey, "Pyrrhonian Skepticism."

75. Burnyeat, "Can the Skeptic Live," 138. In this piece, Burnyeat is arguing for a different thesis—that Sextus's Skepticism is *incoherent*. Yet the two theses (self-refutation and incoherence) are related in that they both concern whether the Skeptic is making any claims to truth.

76. Sextus, PH 1.14.

77. Sextus, PH 1.15.

78. Both Bailey, "Pyrrhonian Skepticism," and McPherran, "Skeptical Homeopathy," have developed interesting arguments in an attempt to save Sextus from this dilemma. I will not go into their arguments here because this issue is peripheral to our main concerns.

79. Sextus, PH 1.191. See also PH 1.202–05.

80. See Burnyeat, "Can the Skeptic Live."

81. See Sextus, M 7.402–08.

82. Sextus never explains his use of the phrase "cancels itself out" (peritrope). He uses it in the following passage:

> (Moreover, even in the act of enunciating the formulae concerning things non-evident—such as the formula "No more (one thing than another)," or the formula "I determine nothing," or any of the others which we shall presently mention,—he does not dogmatize. For whereas the dogmatizer posits the things about which he is said to be dogmatizing as really existent, the Skeptic does not posit these formulae in any absolute sense; for he conceives that, just as the formula "All things are false" asserts the falsity of itself as well as of everything else, as does the formula "Nothing is true," so also the formula "No more" asserts that itself, like all the rest, is "No more (this than that)," *and thus cancels itself along with the rest.* . . . If then, while the dogmatizer posits the matter of his dogma

as substantial truth, the Skeptic enunciates his formulae so that they are virtually cancelled by themselves, he should not be said to dogmatize in his enunciation of them . . . he states what appears to himself and announces his own impression in an undogmatic way, without making any positive assertion regarding external realities (PH 1.14–15, my emphasis).

Apparently Sextus wants to claim both that his formula "No more this than that" is self-refuting as he enunciates it, and that he does not assert it, but merely reports his impression. Two important points need to be made here. First, the formula "No more this than that" seems different from formulae like "All things are false" in an important respect. While "All things are false" is clearly self-refuting, because if it is true then it entails its own falsity (it must be false as well), the formula "No more this than that" is not self-refuting even if it *were* an assertion (which Sextus denies).

To see why, consider the following: Suppose we have two contradictory propositions: (1) X is Y, and (2) It is not the case that X is Y. And suppose further that: (3) There is as much reason to believe any assertion as there is to believe its negation (No more this than that); and suppose that (3) is an assertion (has a truth value) and (3) is true. If (3) is true, then there is another assertion, call it (4), which is the negation of (3) and for which there is as much reason to believe it as there is to believe (3). Let us call this proposition [i.e., that there is as much reason to believe (4) as there is to believe (3)] (5). The truth of (3) cannot make (4) true [thereby making (3) self-refuting]. If (5) is true, then we *cannot know* if (3) is true. Thus, the truth of (3) affects the epistemological relationship between the person asserting (3) and (3), that is, the truth of (3) makes knowledge of (3) impossible, but not being able to know it does not affect its truth. Second, since Sextus denies making any assertions, how could his *impression* "No more this than that" refute itself? I know of no notion of self-refutation that does not require a reference to truth (see Mackie, "Self-Refutation—A Formal Analysis"), and in any case, Sextus refers to truth in the passage cited. See note 78 for other references on this matter.

83. Burnyeat, "Can the Skeptic Live."

84. See Susan Haack, "The Justification of Deduction," *Mind* 85 (January. 1976): 112–19.

85. This is an alternative translation, which seems more appropriate here.

86. Michael de Montaigne, "Apology for Raymond Sebond," in *The Essays of Michael de Montaigne*, tr. and ed. Jacob Zeitlin (New York: Knopf, 1935), 266. For a slightly different translation see the Modern Library Edition, tr. E. Trenchmann (New York: Modern Library, 1946), 522.

87. John Owen, *The Skeptics of the French Renaissance* (London: Swan, Sonnenschein; New York: Macmillan, 1893), 475. At the end of this passage, Owen notes: "This is especially true of portions of the Apology chapter."

88. See R. H. Popkin, *The History of Skepticism from Erasmus to Spinoza* (Berkeley: University of California Press, 1979), 43, who also cites P. Villey, *Sources et Evolution*, I, (Paris: Hachette, 1908), 218 and 365, and II, 164–65.

89. Trenchmann, "Apology for Raymond Sebond," 481.

90. There is some debate about whether his "Apology" was really a defense or an

irreligious parody. See Popkin, chap. 3, and Zeitlin, commentary in *Essays of Michael de Montaigne*, 481–519.

91. For a more extensive account of the history surrounding Montaigne's essay, see Popkin, chap. 3; Zeitlin, II, 481–87; Owen, 423–90.

92. Zeitlin, 266. For an alternate translation, see Trenchmann, 522.

93. Zeitlin, 266.

94. See Sextus, PH 1.16–17, "Has the Skeptic a Doctrinal Rule?"

95. Popkin, 51.

96. This is implied at the end of the essay. (See Zeitlin, 269.) Also, on p. 166, where he speaks of suspending judgment, he speaks of "false sects" in the same sentence.

97. Zeitlin, 225.

98. Zeitlin, 202.

99. Recall from Chapter 1: Proposition P is a pragmatic presupposition of question Q for a person S at time T = def. S takes P to be semantically or conceptually related to Q in such a way that P constitutes at least part of the parameter or framework within which answers to Q count as acceptable kinds of answers. Surely, in asking the question that poses the problem, Montaigne would seem to be pragmatically presupposing that truth and knowledge are also attainable through God. This kind of presupposition, it seems, would count for Montaigne as a proposition that forms at least part of the framework for acceptable answers to his question. This sort of presupposition would not be shared by Sextus and, consequently, their characterizations of the problem of the criterion would be different as well.

100. Cardinal D. J. Mercier, *A Manual of Modern Scholastic Philosophy*, tr. T. L. Parker and S. A. Parker (London: Kegan Paul, Trench, Trubner, 1928), vol. 1, 354. Mercier's translation of the passage is slightly different from Zeitlin's translation cited earlier, but these differences are of no philosophical significance to us.

101. Ibid.

102. Ibid.

103. Ibid., 350; my emphasis.

104. Ibid., 354. Mercier uses "doubt" for a state of suspension of judgment; See 369–70.

105. Ibid., 356.

106. Ibid., 63. Cited from Cardinal D. J. Mercier's *Critèriologie*, 8th ed. (Paris: Felix Alcan, 1923), 234.

107. Ibid.

108. Ibid. Compare with Cardinal Mercier's Manual, 363–65.

109. Mercier, *Manual*, 365.

110. Alan Bailey has an interesting discussion about the self-evident, and how often we mistakenly take something to be obviously self-evident. (See "Pyrrhonian Skepticism," 34–35.)

111. My thanks to Barry Gan for this point.

112. Mercier, Manual, 355.

113. Ibid., 369; author's emphasis.

114. Ibid., 370.
115. Ibid., chap. 4, 377–84.
116. Ibid., 350; my emphasis.
117. Ibid., 370.
118. Ibid., 350; my emphasis.
119. P. Coffey, *Epistemology or Theory of Knowledge*, vol. 1 (London: Longmans, Green, 1917), 144.
120. For example, Mercier's three metacriteria for an acceptable solution are all pragmatic presuppositions not shared by Sextus and Montaigne.

Chapter 3

Nicholas Rescher's Systems-Theoretic Approach

Nicholas Rescher purports to "meet and overcome"[1] the problem of the criterion. In a series of books, Rescher lays down a comprehensive "systems-theoretic approach," part of which is intended as his solution to the problem of the criterion.[2] In this chapter, I will try to determine whether he succeeds in solving this problem. However, I will analyze his "systems-theoretic approach" only insofar as it pertains to the problem of the criterion. A thorough analysis of Rescher's system is far beyond the scope of this inquiry. I will argue that even if we grant Rescher that all of the details of his theory are as unproblematic as he purports them to be, there are still serious problems with his theory, and he has not succeeded in solving the problem of the criterion. Indeed, I will show that Rescher's solution puts us right back on the wheel where we started. Nonetheless, Rescher's approach to the problem of the criterion, I believe, is insightful and extremely valuable in pointing us in the direction of a resolution.

Let us begin by describing what Rescher takes to be the problem of the criterion. He refers to Sextus Empiricus, D. J. Mercier, P. Coffey, and Roderick Chisholm in this regard and quotes Montaigne:

> To Adjudicate [between the true and the false] among the appearances of things we need to have a distinguishing method (un instrument judicatoire); to validate this method we need to have a justifying argument; but to validate this justifying argument we need the very method at issue. And there we are, going round on the wheel.[3]

Rescher seems to have the same argument in mind when he speaks of the problem of the criterion or *diallelus* as we have described in the previous chapter.[4] But Rescher then states that the lesson of this argument is that it is impossible to validate our criterion of truth by somehow directly showing that it "works" at picking out only truths. He states: "It is in principle impossible to make a direct check of this sort on the functioning of our truth-determining methods."[5]

Rescher's interpretation of the wheel argument makes a dogmatic point and is, therefore, unlike my interpretation of Sextus and Montaigne. And if this is what Rescher means by the problem of the criterion (i.e., how can one possibly justify a criterion of truth by using the results obtained from applying the criterion to justify it?), then we can see that, in effect, Rescher is claiming that neither he nor anyone else *can solve* the problem of the criterion. *Solving* the problem of the criterion implies a *showing* that cannot be achieved without employing the very criterion in question in the demonstration. So, as Rescher maintains, the very nature of the problem of the criterion is such that a "showing" is, in principle, impossible. Hence, Rescher could not have "met and overcome" the problem of the criterion—indeed, as he himself claims, a solution is impossible.[6]

If Rescher has not solved the problem of the criterion, then what does he do in his series of books? And, more importantly, is it pertinent to our discussion of "the problem of the criterion"?[7] Would anything short of a demonstrative "showing" be sufficient to "meet and overcome" any of the problems of the criterion that we have discussed? Even if Rescher cannot demonstratively show that some criterion (M) is the true criterion of truth, it would be significant to the problem of the criterion if he could show that we are rationally justified in believing that (M) is true.[8] It would be significant if he could show that we are rationally justified in believing that (M) yields justified beliefs when applied; that is, it would be significant if Rescher could show any of the following:

1. That (M) in fact yields only truths, or
2. That we are justified in believing that (M) yields only truths, or
3. That (M) in fact yields only justified beliefs, or
4. That we are justified in believing that (M) yields only justified beliefs.

However, it seems that in order to show any one of these options, we would need to apply the very criterion (M) in question. For example, suppose that our criterion (M) is:

(M)–S is justified in believing P if S's belief that P is causally derived from sense experience.

Suppose, then, that I apply (M) and conclude that my beliefs x, y, and z are justified on the basis of (M). What then justifies (M)? What justifies our believing (M)? In other words, what justifies our belief that (M) picks out only justified beliefs? Obviously, we cannot employ (M) without circularity, and so we need another criterion to judge it, and that criterion will require another, and so on. Thus, we are led on an infinite regress.

Hence, if Rescher could show that we are rationally justified (warranted) in believing that criterion (M) will yield only true beliefs, or only justified beliefs, he would have done something of considerable import. This would certainly seem to constitute a solution to the problem of the criterion.

Showing any one of the four options would be a justification of that criterion and would settle a dispute; it would be a solution because it would remove rational doubt about the answer to either question (i.e., Rescher's formulation concerning justification or Sextus's version concerning settling a dispute). If he could *show* that (M) yields only justified beliefs, then there would be no more "reasoned" disagreement—no more dispute that has a rational basis. Recall from Chapter 1 that a solution to a problem must be (1) a statement or series of statements, (2) a semantically appropriate response, (3) an answer to the question, (4) true, and it must (5) remove rational doubt. If Rescher could show any one of the four options discussed, then he would meet the necessary and sufficient conditions for a solution by meeting these conditions.

I will begin at the end of Rescher's "system" and see just what he purports to have accomplished. If he provides arguments that he claims give us rational warrant or justification in believing that a certain criterion (M) will, or probably will, lead us to only justified beliefs or true beliefs, then we should examine his arguments in close detail. If his arguments at their best do something short of this, then they may be interesting, but they are irrelevant to our focus of concern.

At some points in his discussion, Rescher seems to claim that he can provide a "systematic noncircular validation for the system of our beliefs as a whole,"[9] that the wheel argument can be "met and overcome . . . by sufficiently careful countermoves."[10] At other points, he seems to claim that the best he can do is to provide a "plausibility argument . . . one that builds a good case for its conclusion, providing it with a solid rational warrant which (admittedly) stops short of giving a logically airtight guarantee."[11]

Rescher's strategy can best be understood as a two-part argument. In the first, part he claims to show that we can be rationally warranted in believing that adopting a certain method will be successful at attaining some specified goal. This can be thought of as his pragmatic justification of a methodology. The details of this discussion are, for the present, unimportant. What is important is what Rescher thinks this discussion shows. He maintains that he has presented an argument for the rational validation (justification) of a practical course of action to attain some specified goal. For example, for some method (M) and some goal (G):

I. (M) works (as well as any envisioned alternative) for realizing (G). Therefore (M) is to be adopted as the correct method relative to (G).[12]

Let us assume, for now, that Rescher can successfully do what he says he has done. This completes the first part of his two-part argument. The second part is a "plausibility argument," which purports to link *pragmatic success with truth*, so that we then become rationally warranted in believing that certain sorts of (M) will not only achieve some goal (G), but further, that the success of (M) at achieving (G) is so linked with truth that pragmatic success establishes (M) as a correct criterion of *truth* as well. Rescher believes that through an argument called "metaphysical deduction" he can show that it is "effectively impossible" for a method (M) to be "systematically" successful at attaining some specified goal (G) and for this method to be an "error-producing cognitive procedure" as well.[13] If every detail of Rescher's two-part argument were to turn out as successful as he claims, he would have as a conclusion that we can be rationally warranted in believing that a method (M) will yield truths. Therefore, we must look more closely at parts of Rescher's discussion to see if his arguments are sound.

Let us adopt the strategy of beginning at the end of Rescher's discussion and working our way into his "system" only as far as we need to go in order to determine how successful are his arguments. By doing this, we may avoid immersing ourselves in details that are irrelevant to our concerns. We will begin by granting Rescher almost all of what he claims, and only question one point at a time, starting with one of his conclusions. A few preliminary remarks are necessary to make this discussion intelligible.

Rescher's overall strategy is that since it is impossible to validate or justify our criterion of factual truth by using the results obtained from applying the criterion to justify it, it is necessary to look for a different kind of justification or validation—one that would somehow avoid the need to employ the criterion in question to justify the criterion, and yet one that would be a strong enough kind of "justifying" or "giving of reasons" to make it at least rationally justifiable to believe that the criterion yields only truths (or justified beliefs).

Rescher's first move, then, is to describe another kind of justification. He chooses pragmatic justification and likens it to Aristotle's practical syllogism.[14] For the present, the details of this discussion are unimportant. This is one part of what Rescher calls his "cycles of justification." This part of the cycle might be represented by the following steps:

Step 1. Begin with a method (M) and goal (G).
Step 2. Apply (M).
Step 3. Note that (M) yields factual theses x, y, and z.
Step 4. Act on x, y, and z.
Step 5. Note whether such action results in achieving goal (G).

Step 6. Success in achieving goal (G) then justifies the use of method (M).

So, unlike a validating argument whose conclusion asserts a *fact*, the conclusion of a pragmatic justification simply *recommends or prescribes* a particular course of *action*. Although Rescher does not discuss specifics, it seems that an example of such a pragmatic justification might look like this:

> Suppose that we are picking tomatoes. We begin with some goal (G) and a method or criterion (M):
> Goal (G): To pick only tomatoes that would nourish me.
> Criterion or Method (M): A tomato is nourishing if it is red, firm, unbruised, and not mouldy.

Now I apply method (M) and (M) yields the factual thesis that tomatoes x, y, and z are nourishing tomatoes. In order to determine whether acting on (M) was "successful," I would not be able to use method (M) to determine success, for this would be circular. But the success of (M) at achieving (G) is pragmatically determined by how well they nourish me. If they do not nourish me then there will be "pangs in my midriff."[15] So the *consequences determine success*; if I am nourished, then this would "justify" me (pragmatically) in believing that if I want to achieve goal (G), I can do so by using method (M). It justifies me in believing that *using* method (M) will result in picking only nourishing tomatoes.

The same line of reasoning would also hold for a criterion of truth. Once we have established the "success" of some method, we can conclude: "If we use the (nonpragmatic) criterion C as basis for classing theses (in general) as true, then this generic process—this general policy—will provide a satisfactory guide to action."[16]

We will assume, for the present time, that all goes well with Rescher's pragmatic justification. Rescher then argues that through what he calls his "metaphysical deduction," he can establish a relationship between pragmatic success and truth, such that if some method (M) is systematically successful at achieving some goal (G), then it is "effectively impossible" for it to be an "error-producing cognitive procedure" as well.[17] This is the second part of what Rescher calls his "cycles of justification." These two parts "lock together" in "spiraling cycles" (like a double helix) of justification; and as Rescher maintains, "Only when everything is adjusted and readjusted so that *all* the pieces fit in a smooth dovetailing, will we obtain a workable pragmatic methodological justification for an inquiry procedure."[18]

Let us assume, for the present, that all goes well with this too, without delving into the details of its inner workings.[19] What then do we now have? Where do we now stand?

Rescher acknowledges that coherence plays a central role in his description of "cycles of justification." He says, "The theoretical aspect of *coherence* plays a central methodological role throughout this cyclic process."[20] This seems to be what he means by saying "*only when* all the pieces fit together in a smooth dovetailing,"[21] that is, only when the "cycle" that involves the pragmatic justification of a method and the "cycle" that involves his "metaphysical deduction," and all the "pieces" involved in each cycle "fit together" do we achieve justification.

So it would seem that coherence is a necessary condition for justification in Rescher's system. It should be noted here that Rescher's "system" differs from that of a modest foundationalist[22] in that at many places Rescher strongly denies that any method or factual thesis has any initial epistemic warrant.[23] Since coherence is a necessary condition of justification in Rescher's system, one might be led to think that for all its complications, Rescher's system is simply a coherence theory of justification (which includes in it a coherence theory of truth as well). If this is true, then Rescher faces three problems; two of the problems are standard objections to coherence theories of justification in general,[24] while the third and most serious problem is peculiar to Rescher's system.

The first may be called the problem of the multiplicity of *equally coherent systems*. The objection is, simply, why can there not be many equally coherent systems, each with a different method, pragmatic justification, metaphysical deduction, and so on, justifying incompatible factual theses? As Bonjour claims, if, in the last analysis, we are only relying on coherence, then it seems that with a little work we could justify anything. For any proposition, it seems that we could build one coherent theory of justification to justify it, and another to justify its negation. Furthermore, we have no way of deciding between conflicting and equally coherent systems of justification, because coherence is our only criterion. This criticism sounds similar to the kinds of claims Sextus made against Stoic claims; for any thesis that the Stoics would put forward, the Skeptics were able to show that its contradictory was equally reasonable, leading them to suspend judgment. Every claim was "No more this than that." If two contradictory claims can be "justified" by equally coherent systems, then we have no reason to prefer one to the other.

The second problem has been termed the "detachment from reality" objection, or the "isolation" objection. Roughly put, the objector argues that from the fact that a system is coherent, it does not follow that the beliefs therein need bear any relationship with reality or the world outside, because justification in a coherent system only consists of relations among parts *within* that system; and because of this feature, we have no way to link it to the "external world," that is, justification is a wholly internal matter. Our intuitions about justification tell us that we need some kind of tether that reaches outside the internals of the system. Justification needs to be somehow connected to truth, be truth-conducive, to be a justification.

There have been a number of improvements and refinements to this objection, which accommodate fallibilist approaches to justification by linking justification to evidence rather than truth.[25] For example, Paul Moser characterizes the objection as:

> IO: Epistemic coherentism entails that one can be epistemically justified in accepting a contingent empirical proposition that is incompatible with, or at least improbable, given one's total empirical evidence.[26]

The third problem is that if Rescher is ultimately relying simply on coherence, then he is right back on the wheel again. We have the problem of the criterion all over again, because we can then pose the question "What justifies you in maintaining that coherence is the necessary method or criterion for arriving at justification?"

Rescher recognizes these objections as problems for ordinary coherence theories, but believes that he has an answer to all three of these problems.[27] He maintains that there is a difference between his coherence theory and all other coherence theories, which makes his theory immune to these objections. His theory of justification does *not depend entirely* upon coherence of all its internal parts, but also relies significantly on *pragmatic success in the world.* He agrees that most of the elements of his system of justification lie *within* our control and manipulation, and thus these elements would be vulnerable to the criticisms above. However, there is one element that is beyond our control—that links the system to the world. It is:

> the *consequences* of our actions; those results which determinate actions bring in their wake. In short, while we can change how we think and act, *the success or failure attendant upon changes is something wholly outside the sphere of our control.* . . . Here we come up against the ultimate, theory-external, thought-exogenously independent variable. Pragmatic success constitutes the finally decisive controlling factor.[28]

This so-called external element is what Rescher calls a "reality principle," which he believes is the tether needed to ground his system of justification.

Indeed, Rescher seems correct in saying that the consequences of our actions are beyond our control. The question, however, is whether this insight does any real work for Rescher in securing his system. The answer, I believe, is that it does not. It is not "consequences" that cohere, but our *beliefs and judgments* about the nature of the consequences that cohere (or do not cohere).²⁹ And our beliefs and judgments about the consequences of some action are very much dependent upon *internal* factors, which we can manipulate and control.

How would Rescher suggest we resolve a dispute about consequences? He cannot rely on coherence in such cases because this route leads back into the problems cited above concerning circular reasoning. What Rescher does say about this is that although we are correct in saying that it is our beliefs that are really at play here, and thus:

> pragmatic success and failure do not feature directly in our belief system, ... the coupling between actual and judged success . . . is so strong that no very serious objection can be supported by pressing hard upon a distinction that makes so little difference.³⁰

But what justifies us in believing in this so-called coupling between a belief and reality? This seems to be another judgment—a belief—which begs the question at hand. Certainly coherence within a system cannot justify it, for that route leads us back into the problems cited above about circular reasoning. How would disputes be resolved here? Rescher's answer is completely unsatisfactory. His "reality principle" seems more like a wish. The following rather simplistic example will illustrate my point:

Suppose again that we are picking tomatoes.
Goal (G): To pick only tomatoes that nourish me.
Criterion or Method (M): A tomato is nourishing if it is red, firm, not bruised, and not moldy.

I apply (M) and pick only red, firm, not bruised, not moldy tomatoes. How do I then judge success? How do I judge whether method (M) actually picked out the good tomatoes? We cannot judge success by seeing if all the tomatoes meet the specifications of (M) (as we noted earlier), but rather we will judge success by some pragmatic concerns. As we said earlier, if they do not nourish me, then, as Rescher explained, there will be "pangs in my midriff."³¹

But, while we can all agree that the consequences determine success, how do we determine the consequences? Obviously, I make a *judgment* about the consequences. Now suppose that we have two people, S1 and S2. They both have goal (G) and both apply method (M) and pick out the same tomatoes, say x, y, and z. They both now want to determine the "success" of (M) at attaining (G). So they both eat x, y, and z. Both have no hunger pangs. S1 maintains that (M) is successful at attaining goal (G) on the basis of her eating x, y, and z. S2 maintains that (M) is a complete failure at attaining goal (G) on the basis of her eating x, y, and z. S2 just thinks she has hunger pangs.

How are we to resolve this dispute? Where is this "coupling" between belief and reality?

The point is not that Rescher has provided us with no way to resolve disputes like this, but rather that there is no necessary "coupling" between belief and reality. Even if there were agreement between S1 and S2, this would show nothing. Agreement does not establish success and disagreement does not establish failure. Rescher really avoids addressing this very serious problem. I imagine that Sextus would have given a response similar to this, were he to have addressed Rescher's argument. (Impressions are one thing, but how things are in reality—in truth—is an altogether different matter.)

Although this example is rather simple, it makes the necessary point. There is no reason to believe that our judgments of success bear any relation to actual success. And thus, there is no reason to believe that our beliefs stand in "close apposition" with the "harsh rulings of external reality."[32]

Therefore, even if we grant Rescher the bulk of his arguments, he is still left vulnerable to the two objections against coherence theories,[33] and more importantly, he is vulnerable to the third objection which places him right back on the wheel. Rescher's "indirect solution" fails to solve the problem of the criterion. However we have learned a valuable lesson from his admirable efforts. Rescher sees that the problem of the criterion is, in principle, impossible to solve, and so he tries to do the next best thing—offer something that comes close. I believe that this general approach is on the right track, but obviously there is an important piece of the puzzle still missing. The next philosopher that we consider, largely responsible for the current revival of interest in the problem of the criterion, may help supply the necessary insights. He is Roderick Chisholm.

NOTES

1. See Rescher, *Scepticism*, 13.

2. Rescher, *The Coherence Theory of Truth* (Oxford: Clarendon Press, 1973); *The Primacy of Practice* (Oxford: Basil Blackwell, 1973); *Methodological Pragmatism* (Oxford: Basil Blackwell, 1977); and *Scepticism*.

3. Michael de Montaigne, "An Apology for Raymond Sebond," in *The Essays of Montaigne*, Bk. II, tr. E. Trenchmann (New York: Modern Library, 1946), 544.

4. Rescher seems to take all of the cited authors to be describing the same problem, whereas I have tried to show that some of the characterizations (e.g., Mercier's) are different.

5. Rescher, *Methodological Pragmatism*, 18.

6. This interpretation of the problem of the criterion seems to be a somewhat different problem from the one attributed to Sextus and Montaigne in Chapter 2. Their

problem concerns settling a dispute about differing claims to truth, while Rescher's concerns justifying a criterion of truth. They are obviously closely related, but whether they turn out to be the same problem will depend upon whether they make the same presuppositions in posing the problem and whether a solution to the one is a solution to the other and vice versa. (See Chapter 1 for my discussion of identity conditions for problems.) It seems clear that a solution to Sextus's problem would be a solution to Rescher's problem—if an irrefutable proof were produced, it would be a satisfactory validation—but it is not completely clear to me whether the kind of "showing" that Rescher describes would satisfy Stoic epistemological standards.

7. I do not mean to suggest that there is only one problem of the criterion called the problem of the criterion; rather, I am referring to problems that historically have been called the problem of the criterion.

8. As Alan Bailey correctly explains, "Moreover it is also clear that the five tropes set out by Sextus call into question our claims to **rationally justified belief** as well as our claims to knowledge" ("Pyrrhonian Skepticism," 29, my emphasis).

9. Rescher, *Scepticism*, 13. In his more recent work, *Rationality*, Rescher seems to reject the possibility of noncircular validation for our system of beliefs. There he argues that any such justification must be circular, but is not viciously circular.

> Admittedly, the reasoning at issue has an appearance of vitiating circularity because the force of the argument itself rests on an appeal to rationality: "If you are going to be rational in your beliefs, then you must also act rationally, because it is rational to believe that rational action is optimal in point of goal attainment." But this sort of question begging is simply unavoidable in the circumstances. It is exactly what we want and need. Where else should we look for a rational validation of rationality but to reason itself? The only reasons for being rational that it makes sense to ask for are rational reasons. . . . That presupposition of rationality is not vitiating, not viciously circular, but essential—an unavoidable consequence of the self-sufficiency of cognitive reason. There is simply no satisfactory alternative to using reason in its own defence. . . . Given the very nature of the justificatory enterprise at issue, one just cannot avoid letting rationality sit in judgement of itself" [*Rationality* (Oxford: Clarendon Press, 1988), 43–44].

This change in his position, however, will not satisfy the skeptic, as Rescher himself acknowledges: "Such argumentation will not of course satisfy the skeptic. For him, the lack of guarantees undermines the whole project of rationality" (p. 47).

10. Rescher, *Scepticism*, 13.
11. Rescher, *Methodological Pragmatism*, 97.
12. Rescher, *Primacy of Practice*, 5.
13. Rescher, *Methodological Pragmatism*, 90.
14. Rescher, *Primacy of Practice*, 5.
15. See Rescher, "Reply to Bonjour," in *The Philosophy of Nicholas Rescher*, ed. E. Sosa (Dordrecht, Holland: Reidel, 1979), 174.
16. Rescher, *Primacy of Practice*, 7.
17. Rescher, *Methodological Pragmatism*, 90.
18. Rescher, *Methodological Pragmatism*, 107.
19. Rescher's metaphorical description makes it difficult to determine precisely

what he means, and how this justification is supposed to actually work, for example, "double helix of justification," and "smooth dovetailing." But we may not need to press this issue if there are other problems ahead.

20. Rescher, *Methodological Pragmatism*, 125.

21. Rescher, *Methodological Pragmatism*, 107.

22. Modest foundationalism, roughly speaking, is the thesis that some of our beliefs have at least some initial epistemic warrant.

23. See Rescher, *Coherence Theory*, 207–10, 316–33.

24. See L. Bonjour, "Rescher's Epistemological System," in *Philosophy of Nicholas Rescher*, 168; and E. Sosa, "Foundations of Foundationalism," Nous 14 (Nov. 1980): 547–64; and J. Cornman, *Skepticism, Justification and Explanation* (Dordrecht, Holland: Reidel 1980).

25. See Paul Moser, "Lehrer's Coherentism and the Isolation Objection," in *The Current State of the Coherence Theory*, ed. John Bender (Dordrecht, Holland: Kluwer, 1989), 29–37; also E. Sosa, "The Raft and the Pyramid," in *Midwest Studies in Philosophy, V, Studies in Epistemology*, ed. P. French, T. Uehling, and H. Wettstein (Minneapolis: University of Minnesota Press, 1980), 3–25.

26. Paul Moser, "Lehrer's Coherentism," 33.

27. Because we are mainly concerned with this third objection, and because Rescher himself sees all three objections as valid objections to coherence theories, we need not open a discussion here about how serious is, for example, the multiplicity of equally coherent systems objection.

28. Rescher, *Methodological Pragmatism*, 108.

29. Bonjour makes this point in "Rescher's Epistemological System," 169.

30. Rescher, "Reply to Bonjour," 174.

31. Ibid.

32. Ibid., 173.

33. This is because we have shown that he has not provided the "tether" for his system that would make him immune to such objections. Even if Rescher were to find a way around the first two standard objections to coherence theories of justification, his main difficulty lies with the third objection. Keith Lehrer offers a response to Moser's version of the isolation objection in "Reply to My Critics," in *Current State of the Coherence Theory*, 258–59.

Chapter 4

Roderick Chisholm and the Problem of the Criterion

THE PROBLEM

The current revival of interest in the problem of the criterion can, in great part, be attributed to Roderick Chisholm. As early as 1957, Chisholm addressed the problem in *Perceiving*. A modified treatment can be found later in *Theory of Knowledge*, and a more recent modification can be found in *The Foundations of Knowing*.[1] This latest characterization first appeared as the Aquinas lecture of 1973.[2] Chisholm begins his lecture with these words:

> "The problem of the criterion" seems to me to be one of the most important and one of the most difficult of all the problems of philosophy. I am tempted to say that one has not begun to philosophize until one has faced this problem and recognized how unappealing, in the end, each of the possible solutions is.[3]

In this chapter, I will evaluate how well Chisholm has "faced" this problem, and assess how satisfactory is his "unappealing" solution. I take Chisholm's latest treatment in *FK* to be definitive of his current position.[4] Chisholm begins his explanation of the problem with a paraphrase of Montaigne:

> To know whether things really are as they seem to be, we must have a *procedure* for distinguishing appearances that are true from appearances that are false. But to know whether our procedure is a good procedure, we have to know whether it really *succeeds* in distinguishing appearances that are true from appearances that are false. And we cannot know whether it does really succeed unless we already know which appearances are *true* and which ones are *false*. And so we are caught in a circle.[5]

We can formulate this account into two principles:

1. To know true appearances (things that are as they appear) from false appearances (things that are not as they appear), we need a procedure to distinguish them.

2. To know a good distinguishing procedure from a bad distinguishing procedure, we need already to know which appearances are true and which appearances are false.

One might, then, formulate this problem as follows:
If one does not have prior knowledge of a correct procedure for distinguishing true appearances from false ones, how can one possibly know which appearances are true and which are false? And, if one does not have prior knowledge of which appearances are true and which are false, how can one possibly know which procedure for distinguishing true from false appearances is a correct procedure?

At this point it is difficult to determine whether Chisholm is describing the same or a different problem than Montaigne and Sextus Empiricus. I will address this question at the end of this chapter. In any event, posing the questions in this way seems to presuppose a principle of epistemic priority that I would characterize as:

EP: Temporally prior knowledge of true appearances and false appearances is necessary to determine or recognize a correct procedure for distinguishing true from false appearances, and temporally prior knowledge of a correct procedure for distinguishing true from false appearances is necessary for knowledge of true appearances and false appearances.

This principle, of course, might be disputed by a coherentist, for surely it is possible that knowledge of true and false appearances may come into existence simultaneously with knowledge of correct distinguishing procedures for true and false appearances. This is a possibility that Chisholm does not consider and is worthy of further investigation later (see Chapter 5).

Chisholm asks what a satisfactory solution to this problem would look like and cites Cardinal Mercier's *Critèriologie* for his answer. Looking back on our explanation in Chapter 2, we see that Mercier claimed a criterion of truth should satisfy three conditions: "it must be *internal, objective and immediate.*"[6] This is a metacriterion for acceptable criteria of truth. Do we have any rational grounds for accepting or rejecting this metacriterion? And does Chisholm endorse this metacriterion? As I stated in Chapter 2, Mercier's arguments for these criteria are unconvincing, and most importantly, are subject to the very problem he is trying to solve. In other words, how do we know that this metacriterion is a good metacriterion for distinguishing good criteria of truth from false criteria of truth? It seems as if we need to already know a good criterion of truth to test the merit of this metacriterion. We seem to be back on the wheel at this metalevel.

Chisholm is actually quite careful not to endorse explicitly Cardinal Mercier's position. He simply cites Mercier with no evaluation of the Cardinal's claims. At the end of his analysis, Chisholm notes that his solution to the problem of the criterion is consistent with Mercier's metacriterion. He never states that Mercier has it right, only that his solution is compatible with Mercier's conditions. If Chisholm did endorse Mercier's metacriterion, then he would be vulnerable to the same criticisms that have been levied against Mercier. And in addition to these criticisms, Chisholm would be vulnerable to another criticism. The metacriterion conflicts with claims that Chisholm makes during his explanation of the problem:

> If we could fix on a good method for distinguishing between good and bad methods, we might be all set. But this, of course, just moves the problem to a different level. How are we to distinguish between a good method for choosing good methods? If we continue in this way, of course, we are led to an infinite regress and we will never have an answer to our original question.[7]

Chisholm recognizes the problem involved in "fixing on a method," and this is why I believe he does not explicitly endorse Mercier's metacriterion. But the success or failure of Chisholm's main discussion of the problem of the criterion can be assessed independent of the question of whether he accepts Mercier's metacriterion.

Chisholm sets out to illustrate the problem of the criterion with the help of Descartes's reply to the seventh set of objections to his *Meditations*.[8] In this reply, Descartes is defending his method of doubt by comparing the mind "to a basket containing good and bad apples."[9]

> Supposing he had a basket of apples and fearing that some of them were rotten, wanted to take those out lest they might make the rest go wrong, how could he do that? Would he not first turn the whole of the apples out of the basket and look them over one by one, and then having selected those which he saw not be rotten, place them again in the basket and leave out the others?[10]

Peter Coffey interprets this simile as: "By what test are we to discern the true from the false? This is the problem of the criterion."[11] There is a subtle difference between asking how we know true appearances from false appearances and asking by what test we are to discern the true from the false. For now let us simply label them version 1 and version 2 and proceed with Chisholm's interpretation. He takes the simile to mean:

> But how are we to do the sorting? If we are to sort out the good ones from the bad ones, then, of course, we must have a way of recognizing the good ones. Or

at least we must have a way of recognizing the bad ones . . . in the case of beliefs, we do not have a method or criterion for distinguishing the good ones from the bad ones. Or, at least we don't have one yet. . . . And now, you see, we are on the wheel. First we want to find out which are the good beliefs and which are the bad ones. To find this out we have to have some way—some method—of deciding which are the good ones and which are the bad ones. But there are good and bad methods—good and bad ways—of sorting out the good beliefs from the bad ones. And so now we have a new problem: How are we to decide which are the good methods and which are the bad ones? . . . It can only be that we already know how to tell the difference between the good beliefs and the bad ones . . . [and] if you can *see* which ones are the good ones and which ones are the bad ones, why do you think you need a general method for sorting them out?[12]

This interpretation seems to be concerned with how we do the sorting, that is, how we sort out cases of knowledge from cases that only appear to be knowledge—call it version 3. Version 3 need not involve a test, although Chisholm's claims about "having some way—some method" for sorting seem to commit him to it. Chisholm speaks of these three versions interchangeably, which indicates to me that he *takes* all three questions to pose the same problem and all three questions to involve the same pragmatic presuppositions. Whether these questions do all pose the same problem is an issue we will deal with shortly.

When Chisholm speaks of "finding out"—which beliefs are good and which are bad—he seems to mean "to know" or "to determine." Hence, it is not surprising when Chisholm then summarizes the philosophical issues involved in this problem by two pairs of questions:

(A) *What* do we know? What is the *extent* of our knowledge?
(B) How are we to decide *whether* we know? What are the *criteria* of knowledge?[13]

He suggests that if we had an answer to (A), then we might be able to fashion an answer to (B) on the basis of (A). Also, if we had an answer to (B), then we might be able to fashion an answer to (A) on the basis of (B).

According to Chisholm, philosophers' opinions have divided three ways with respect to this problem. One group purports to know the answer to (A), that is, they purport to know what particular things we do know, and on the basis of this, they fashion a criterion in accord with their answer. Chisholm names this group *particularists*. They include common-sense philosophers, such as Thomas Reid, G. E. Moore, and Chisholm himself. Another group claims to know the answer to (B), that is, they claim to know what the criterion for knowledge is, and on the basis of their answer to (B), they are able to fashion an answer to (A). By knowing the answer to (B), they are able to distinguish true cases of knowledge from those that are merely apparent cases of knowledge. Chisholm calls this group *methodists*. They include such philosophers as Descartes and such empiricists as Hume and Locke. The third group are those who claim that you cannot answer (A) until you know the answer to (B), and you cannot answer (B) until you know the answer to (A). Therefore, you cannot answer either pair of questions. "You cannot know what, if anything, you know, and there is no possible way for you to decide in any particular case."[14] Chisholm calls this group *skeptics*.[15]

The skeptic's position can be formulated as version 4 of the problem of the criterion: If you cannot answer (A) until you know the answer to (B), and if you cannot answer (B) until you know the answer to (A), then how can you answer either question? Since Chisholm speaks of these various versions interchangeably, it seems fair to assume that he takes all of them to have the same pragmatic presuppositions, that is, he takes for granted the same propositions when he considers the various versions of the problem that we have identified. Furthermore, it seems to me that if we had a solution to any one of the versions identified, we would have a solution to all the other versions as well. Hence, we can take all the questions we heretofore identified as different versions of the problem of the criterion *as posing the same problem* for Chisholm. Let us take this last way of posing the problem as paradigmatic of the problem that Chisholm characterizes.

CHISHOLM'S OBJECTIONS TO METHODISM

In this essay, Chisholm never offers any reasons why he finds the skeptic's position unacceptable, except to claim that his approach has one thing in favor of it that the others do not—"the fact that we *do* know many things, after all."[16] This statement, by itself, amounts to the bare claim that skepticism is false and he is correct. To be sure, if Chisholm is correct here, then this would be enough reason to reject skepticism. Yet he expends much more effort to demonstrate why methodism has it wrong.

He begins with a criticism of methodism, and of empiricism in particular. He has two objections. The first applies to all forms of methodism.

1. "The criterion is very broad and far reaching and at the same time completely arbitrary."[17]

Chisholm explains this objection as follows:

How can one *begin* with a broad generalization? . . . He leaves us completely in the dark so far as concerns what *reasons* he may have for adopting this particular criterion rather than some other.[18]

The second objection applies only to empiricism.

2. "When we apply the empirical criterion . . . we seem to throw out not only the bad apples but the good ones as well, and we are left, in effect, with just a few parings or skins with no meat behind them."[19]

In other words, if we apply the empirical criterion, the only things that turn out to count as cases of knowledge are present sensations: "Thus Hume virtually conceded that . . . the only matters of fact that you can really know about pertain to the existence of sensations."[20] The empirical criterion referred to here is "whether [a belief] is derived from sense experience . . . whether it bears certain relations to your sensations."[21] And that position, according to Chisholm, sounds like nonsense. Chisholm explains that the common sense philosophers like Reid and G. E. Moore would contend that any philosophy that implies that we cannot know things (e.g., that this is a hand) should be rejected immediately. He states: "I think that Reid and Moore are right, myself, and I'm inclined to think that the methodists are wrong."[22]

Let us evaluate Chisholm's criticisms of methodism and empiricism. In his first objection, which is directed at all forms of methodism, he claims that the criterion is very broad and far reaching and at the same time completely arbitrary. How do we interpret these two claims? I suggest four possible interpretations:

1. He might be claiming that the *broadness and far-reaching character* of a criterion, in itself, is something to be avoided. But I cannot imagine why. On the contrary, these qualities seem desirable because they suggest that the criterion would be applicable to many cases. Thus, we can reject this first interpretation.

2. He might be claiming that we should avoid *arbitrarily* beginning anything. There must be *reasons* given for adopting this criterion over other possible criteria. Thus, this interpretation of Chisholm's criticism could be avoided if the methodist gives us some reason for adopting his criterion over others. It is the *arbitrariness* that is the issue in this interpretation. Certainly the methodist would be able to afford us *some* reasons for his choice. A methodist would possibly reply that he is not arbitrarily beginning with a broad

and far-reaching criterion. This criterion is known a priori. Certainly having a priori knowledge of a particular criterion is a *reason* for adopting such a criterion, but perhaps his reason would strike Chisholm as a bad reason because it is simply false. Nonetheless, this interpretation of Chisholm's objection to methodism claims that if the adoption of a criterion is *completely arbitrary*, then the methodists have offered us *no* reasons for their adoption of this particular criterion as opposed to some other criterion: "He leaves us completely in the dark so far as concerns what *reasons* he may have for adopting this particular criterion rather than some other."[23] Thus, if it is true that the methodists indeed offer *no* reason to adopt their criterion, then they would be vulnerable to this criticism.

3. He might be claiming that we should avoid adopting a criterion with these two particular characteristics in combination: (a) broad and far-reaching, and (b) arbitrary. On this interpretation, it is somehow the *combination* of "broad and far-reaching" with "arbitrary" that is deadly. But if this is his objection, then he has given us no reason why *this combination* in particular is problematic. If there is some *additional* problem over and above the difficulties mentioned in 1 and 2 above, which arises from this particular combination of characteristics, then it is incumbent upon Chisholm to tell us what this difficulty is. And Chisholm offers no such explanation. I can see no reason why the *combination* presents an especially vexing problem over and above the sum of the problems involved in each. And without such an explanation from Chisholm, this interpretation comes to no more than 1 and 2. One might argue that a broad arbitrary assumption is more irrational than a narrow arbitrary assumption, but this does not seem necessarily so. The content of what is assumed in each case may be the determining factor in deciding which is more irrational.

4. He might be claiming that we simply cannot justifiably *begin* with a *criterion* because it always presupposes some knowledge of particulars to determine whether it succeeds in distinguishing between true and false cases of knowledge. This seems to come to half of the skeptic's claim that in order to answer (B) we already need an answer to (A). This interpretation comes from focusing on Chisholm's stress on the word "begin" in "How can one *begin* with a broad generalization?"[24] The reason why Chisholm finds this question compelling (so this interpretation argues) is that it is puzzling how the methodist can *begin* with a criterion, when such a criterion always seems to presuppose *some* knowledge of particulars to determine whether it really succeeds in distinguishing between true and false cases of knowledge.

It is not clear from what Chisholm states just which interpretation he means to express by his objection. He seems to conflate aspects of the second and fourth interpretations as possible criticisms of methodism. Rather than trying to defend methodism here, let us wait and see if Chisholm's positive thesis, particularism, avoids the very criticism he levies against methodism. For if both positions, particularism and methodism, are vulnerable to his criticism, then, as far as the criticism is concerned, we would have no reason to favor one over the other. But before reviewing his positive thesis let us examine his second objection against methodism, one that is aimed more narrowly just at empiricism.

Chisholm claims that by adopting empiricism we not only throw out the bad apples, but the good ones as well. But how can Chisholm claim this without *assuming* that either his particularist position is the correct one, or at least that knowledge extends farther than the empiricist's position allows (which is also an assumption about what, in fact, we do know)? In other words, Chisholm seems to be assuming an answer to the very question at issue by having assumed already which apples are bad and which are good. He is criticizing empiricism for adopting a criterion that does not agree with his *assumed* position. The very point that we are trying to establish is which apples are bad and which are good, and appeal to such a particularist position (which is, in essence, what his assumption amounts to), simply will not do. Chisholm is *assuming* that he already knows the answer to (A) in order to criticize the empiricist's answer to (B). If this kind of faulty reasoning is allowed for Chisholm, then it is also allowed for the empiricist. The empiricist can then argue that Chisholm's position is unacceptable because it leads one to adopt a "bad" criterion, one that conflicts with the empiricist's intuitions about methods and rules [thereby assuming an answer to (B) in order to criticize Chisholm's answer to (A)]. It forces us to accept bad apples!

Hence, we can reject Chisholm's second objection on the grounds that it assumes an answer to the issue in question, in order to answer the issue in question. Indeed, Chisholm admits that he begs the question, and believes that only by doing so can anyone "deal with the problem." I will return to this question shortly, but for now let us assume that begging the question is a good reason to reject Chisholm's second objection.

PARTICULARISM

We can now examine Chisholm's positive thesis and determine whether his position is vulnerable to either interpretation 2 or 4 of his first objection to methodism. He says:

> I would say—and many reputable philosophers would disagree with me—that to find out whether you know such a thing as that this is a hand, you don't have to

apply any test or criterion. Spinoza had it right. "In order to know" he said, "there is no need to know that we know, much less to know that we know that we know."[25]

Chisholm adopts the particularist's thesis and denies the skeptic's claim that in order to answer (A) we must first answer (B). As he states: "There are many things that quite obviously we do know to be true."[26] And from this he concludes that "having these apples before us, we can look them over and formulate certain criteria of goodness."[27] This is the particularist thesis.

Chisholm's positive thesis, however, seems somewhat garbled. Just exactly what he means by "to find out whether you know" is unclear, but he seems to be equating it with "to know" in his second statement, because his second statement reads like a reiteration of the first: "Spinoza has it right. 'In order to know,' he said, 'there is no need to know that we know, much less know that we know that we know.' "[28] Any other reading of "to find out whether you know" makes this passage completely confusing.

However, to add to this confusion, Chisholm also seems to be conflating two different ideas. His first claim is that "to find out whether you know such a thing as that this is a hand, you don't have to apply any test or criterion." His second claim is that in order to know there is no need to know that you know. Even if I am correct in interpreting "to find out whether you know" as simply "to know" (thereby making the subject of his two claims identical, i.e., both claims are about what is necessary or not necessary "to know," and thus making sense of how these two sentences relate to each other), the two claims assert completely different theses. His two claims read:

1. In order to know, you don't have to apply any test or criterion.
2. In order to know, there is no need to know that you know.

The first claims that applying a test or criterion is not necessary in order to know something, while the second claims that second order knowledge (knowledge about knowledge) is not necessary in order to know, that is, is not necessary for first order knowledge. Possession of second order knowledge is quite different from applying a test or criterion. Chisholm makes the two claims as if to assert the same thesis. Two criticisms are in order here. One concerns the confused statement of his positive thesis, while the other concerns how his positive thesis relates to his criticisms of methodism. I shall discuss his positive thesis first.

If we assume, for the moment, that by "to find out whether we know" Chisholm simply means "to know," then both statements he makes are concerned with what is necessary to know something. It seems clear that we may be able to know something without knowing that we know it.[29] And so, I am in agreement here with Spinoza and Chisholm.[30] But this brings us no closer to a solution to the problem of the criterion, for the same claim can be made by the methodist. One need not know that one knows some criterion to be a correct criterion for sorting the true from the false in order to know some correct criterion.

Therefore, it seems that it is quite a different thing to speak about what is required to find out whether we know something than simply to know it. How can we find out whether we know such a thing, unless we have some kind of criterion for distinguishing such things from things that are not such things? "Finding out whether we know," when *not* understood as simply knowing, is what Chisholm needs to solve the problem. Finding out whether we know something seems to require more than what is required to simply know something. It seems to require some kind of *determination* that is not required for simple knowing because it is a determining or knowing *about* knowledge.

Yet Chisholm has an answer, of sorts, to this. He has made the following three statements:

1. There are many things that quite obviously we do know to be true.[31]
2. And in favor of our approach there is the fact that we do know many things after all.[32]
3. But our view is no more arbitrary than either of the others. And unlike them, it corresponds with what we do know.[33]

Chisholm seems to be saying that in some cases we can find out whether we know something simply by knowing it. The quotes above, then, would be interpreted as: (1) "There are many things that quite obviously (i.e., we have found out) we do know to be true"; and (2) "And in favor of our approach there is the fact (i.e., we have found out) that we do know many things after all." The methodist, however, can use the same strategy to argue that we can find out whether some method works simply by knowing it. This line of argumentation, by itself, puts Chisholm's position in no better standing than the position of the methodist. In effect, this strategy involves *presupposing* the approach one is attempting to establish. As Chisholm states:

> But in all of this I have presupposed the approach I have called "particularism." The "methodist" and "skeptic" will tell us that we have started in the wrong place. If now we try to reason with them, I am afraid, we will be back on the wheel.[34]

What is puzzling is that Chisholm thinks that only by doing so, can he "deal with the problem." "What few philosophers have had the courage to recognize is this: we can deal with the problem only by begging the question."[35] This is a rather puzzling statement because it prompts one to wonder what Chisholm might mean by "deal" with the problem. Perhaps a passage from *Perceiving* will give us a clue. There he states:

> We cannot "test" every mark of evidence in this way unless we reason in a circle. But even if we do thus reason in a circle, we may take some comfort if by doing so we find that induction does not discredit the marks of evidence of its premises.[36]

I believe that what Chisholm is saying is that by begging the question we "deal" with the problem insofar as we can take some comfort if our theory—particularism—does not conflict with what we ordinarily take ourselves to know. But we could take no comfort in the fact that our circular reasoning did not conflict with what we are trying to establish because circular reasoning will not allow such conflicts; that is what is wrong with such reasoning; anything can be so "proven." If this is what Chisholm means by "deal" with the problem, then one criticism is in order. The fact that he begs the question is completely independent of the fact that what he sets out to test corresponds with what we ordinarily take ourselves to know. He could "take comfort" that his reasoning does not conflict with what we ordinarily take ourselves to know even if his reasoning did not beg the question. It just so happens that particularism coincides with common sensism, and that is a fact that is independent of the fact that Chisholm believes that we can only deal with the problem by begging the question.

The only other interpretation of "deal" with the problem that comes to mind is one in which "deal" is not a success word. "Dealing" with the problem, then, is not a solution. But the only avenue open to *any* of the respondents—particularists, methodists, and skeptics—is to beg the question in favor of their position. And so, if begging the question is "dealing" with the problem, then the methodist has the same recourse open to him. The methodist could claim that his view is no more arbitrary than either of the others, and his view corresponds with what we do know (i.e., what are true methods).

Chisholm's position does have the merit of corresponding to what we ordinarily take ourselves to know, but one could certainly question whether this is a merit. Indeed, throughout history many of the things we ordinarily took ourselves to know have been shown to be in error. Aristotle believed that a heavier stone would fall faster than a lighter one. It was common sense. And it was hundreds of years before this belief was empirically tested and shown to be false. So it is questionable whether this is really a merit of Chisholm's position. Furthermore, this merit only sets him apart from the empiricist, not all methodists. There is nothing about methodism that precludes the possibility of its coinciding with our common sense beliefs.

Hence, we can question Chisholm's positive thesis not only on the grounds given above—that none of his arguments in favor of particularism is convincing; that his arguments give us no good reason to prefer particularism over methodism and skepticism—but also because if my interpretation 4 of his objection to methodism is correct, then his own position is subject to the very same objection,—that he is just "beginning" with particularism. We can now see that since Chisholm's position deals with the problem only by begging the question, the methodist can argue, as Chisholm concedes, that we simply cannot begin with a particular, because it always presupposes some knowledge of a method or criterion to determine whether it is a case of true knowledge or merely apparent knowledge; this is the other half of the skeptic's claim that in order to answer (A) we already need an answer to (B).

It seems that Chisholm's last recourse is to appeal to interpretation 2 of his objection to methodism, for if his position is immune to his criticism of methodism under this interpretation, then at least he can claim that his position has this advantage over methodism. Recall that on this interpretation of his objection it is the *arbitrariness* of methodism that is at issue. And on this point, Chisholm himself concedes that his position is no more arbitrary than the others. If *all* he can claim is that his position is no more arbitrary than the others, then he cannot claim that his position is *less* arbitrary. And if he cannot even make the claim that his position is somewhat less arbitrary than the others, then his only remaining objection to methodism—interpretation 2—is just as effective against his own position as it is against methodism. In other words, if it is true that we should avoid arbitrarily beginning with anything, and the most that Chisholm can say is that particularism is no more arbitrary than methodism or skepticism, then particularism is also vulnerable to his criticism of methodism. And it seems that Chisholm cannot argue that his position is less arbitrary (as he apparently recognizes) without, as Chisholm says, going right back on the wheel. In effect, all that he is left with is his claim that his position has it right, and alas, each of the other views can claim just as much of their positions.

We have discovered, then, that Chisholm's solution to the problem of the criterion is more than "unappealing," it is unsatisfactory because (1) he has given us no good reason to reject the other positions, (2) he has given us no good argument to favor his position over the others, and (3) his position begs the question.

If Chisholm concedes that he has *presupposed* particularism, then it seems that what he means by "start with particular cases" is presuppose the truth of particularism, that is, presuppose the truth of particular cases. And indeed, the methodist is doing the very same thing with his criterion or method. He is presupposing the truth of the particular distinguishing principles. Both positions seem question begging because they both presuppose the truth of the position they are trying to show solves the problem. Thus, *if* we assume the truth of particularism, then we have a solution to the problem of the criterion, and *if* we assume the truth of methodism, then we also have a solution. Chisholm's criticisms of methodism and skepticism are his way of arguing that his question begging and arbitrary solution is preferable to its alternatives, which are also question begging and arbitrary.[37]

It is somewhat puzzling that Chisholm then says, "If now we try to reason with them, then, I am afraid, we will be back on the wheel." What is puzzling is the "if." He already admitted that he has presupposed the truth of particularism. Thus, he is already on a wheel. He seems to think that if he does not try to reason with the methodist and skeptic, then he will *not* be back on the wheel. How could this be possible? Only if his proposed solution is not circular. If it is true that he can find out whether he knows such a thing as that this is a hand without applying any test or criterion, then it is true that he *can* answer (A) before or without answering (B). And *answering* (A) does not, by itself, beg the question. I believe that this is what Chisholm is saying when he characterizes his solution as a "kind of answer to the puzzle about the diallelus." By answering (A), he has provided a *kind* of answer to the puzzle without begging the question.

But two things can be said about this answer: (1) the methodist can do the same as well. If it is true that he can find out whether he knows some criterion without looking to any particulars, then it is true that he *can* answer (B) before or without answering (A). And *answering* (B) does not, by itself, beg the question. This is also a *kind* of answer to the puzzle; and (2) neither kind of answer is a *solution* to the problem of the criterion because a solution must remove the initial rational doubt about which position is rationally preferable.

For these reasons we can also claim that there are no good grounds to think that begging the question can ever be a rational means of dealing with the problem. Chisholm's position offers an answer to the question "Is a criterion necessary to adjudicate between the true and the false?" Chisholm's answer is "no." If he could remove rational doubt about his answer—if he could show it to be rationally preferable to the other positions (thereby removing the rational doubt about which answer is correct)—then his answer would be a solution to the problem of the criterion. But this has not been established.

In 1988, Chisholm responded to my criticisms with the following points:

1. Chisholm's arguments for particularism do not constitute a solution to the problem of the criterion: "[W]hat I have said positively about the problem is *not* intended as a solution to the problem."[38] Hence, when Chisholm speaks of "dealing" with the problem, "deal" is not being used as a success word; it does not mean "successfully deal" with the problem. Chisholm believes that "the problem of the criterion *has* no solution."[39]

2. His arguments for particularism do not preclude the possibility of developing a more satisfactory methodist position. There is nothing *in principle* more epistemically satisfactory about particularism than methodism. He states: "we should be open to the possibility that some day the 'methodist' might work out an answer that will take us farther than traditional empiricism has done."[40]

These claims are consistent with the points I have made and lessen the extent of our disagreements. Yet Chisholm also reiterates his particularist position in an effort to explain how his position is an "approach" to the problem. Particularism does give him a way to answer the question "Is a criterion necessary to adjudicate between the true and the false?" Chisholm claims that despite the "insoluble problem of the criterion,"[41] he cannot stop himself from *trying* to answer questions, such as:

> What can I know? How can I distinguish those things that I am justified in believing from those things I am not justified in believing? What can I do to replace unjustified beliefs by justified beliefs that pertain to the same subject matter? What can I do to replace less justified beliefs by more justified beliefs? And—the most puzzling question of all is this: How can I reasonably *decide* how to go about doing these things?[42]

Chisholm claims that particularism gives him a way to provide answers to these questions that *seem to him* "reasonably satisfactory"[43] and that it *seems to him* that by taking either of the other two approaches—methodism and skepticism—one cannot make any "progress at all."[44]

Of course, the methodist and skeptic can make exactly the *same* claims, for they also believe that they can provide answers to the aforementioned questions that *seem to them* "reasonably satisfactory." Both the methodist and the skeptic would aver that by taking either of the other approaches, *it seems to them*, one cannot make any "progress at all." What constitutes "progress" and a "more satisfactory" way to work things out, it seems, depends upon which position one presupposes as true. The conclusion we must draw from this is that Chisholm has not succeeded in showing particularism to be rationally preferable to methodism or skepticism.

CHISHOLM AND SEXTUS

Is the problem of the criterion that Chisholm characterizes, the same or different from the problem that Sextus Empiricus characterizes? The fact that he cites Montaigne as his main source on the problem is evidence that he *takes* himself to be considering the same problem raised by Montaigne and, I might add, Sextus Empiricus.[45] We know that their stated problems concern how one settles a dispute between those who claim certain impressions true or false and those who disagree. We also know that Sextus poses the problem within the context of Stoic epistemology and its condition of irrefutable provability for settlement of such disputes, and that while Montaigne seems to concur with Sextus on these details, we have found reasons to believe that his presuppositions are somewhat different from those of Sextus.[46] These differences can be accounted for in terms of Montaigne's adherence to the tenets of Christianity. Sextus's portrayal makes the problem of the criterion a metaepistemological problem because it concerns what is required to settle a dispute *about knowledge claims.*

Is Chisholm's problem of the criterion an epistemological or metaepistemological problem? Which of the following describes the problem of the criterion:

1. If knowledge of particulars presupposes knowledge of criteria, and vice versa, how can we have knowledge of either? (an *epistemological* problem)
2. If knowledge of knowledge of particulars presupposes knowledge of criteria, and vice versa, how can we have knowledge of either? (a *metaepistemological* problem)

Could Chisholm's characterization be interpreted either way? When he speaks about "finding out whether we know" the problem sounds metaepistemological, and when he agrees with Spinoza that in order to know we need not know that we know, the problem sounds epistemological.

Ernest Sosa sees it as a metaepistemological problem:

> Particularism and methodism are meta-epistemological positions, for they tell us which justifies which of two sorts of *epistemic* knowledge. They tell us whether our knowledge of certain epistemic principles is based on our knowledge that we have bits of knowledge of a certain related kind (e.g., of the external world, that I have two hands), or whether, conversely, our knowledge of a particular kind rests on our knowledge of certain related epistemic principles.[47]

I think Sosa is right here. To see why, let us consider what is required to made a judgment or adjudication of the true from the false and what is required to settle the dispute between the particularist, methodist, and skeptic. Chisholm seems to assume that what is required to make a judgment or adjudication of the true from the false is the same as what is required to know. And as we know, Chisholm claims that we can do this without applying any criterion or method. We can adjudicate between the true and the false—we can know—we can find out whether we know—without applying any test or criterion. This fits in with his theory of evidence and self-presenting states. Since there are certain states that are self-presenting, no application of a criterion or method is necessary to know such a state to be true.

We have discussed *this issue* at length and found that Chisholm's arguments in favor of this position give us no good reason to prefer it over that of the methodist or skeptic. Furthermore, his answers will not settle the dispute between the particularist, methodist, and skeptic for they beg the question. What is required to settle the dispute has not yet been determined. Chisholm's answer is that it cannot be settled—the problem of the criterion has no solution. But the real problem of the criterion here concerns, again, settling a dispute about knowledge claims, and hence, is again a metaepistemological problem.

Chisholm attempts to answer some of the epistemological questions with his particularist position, while at the same time claiming that we can only beg the question when it comes to dealing with the metaepistemological problem of the criterion: "If we now try to reason with them, then, I am afraid, we will be back on the wheel."[48] Simply answering (A) or (B) does not deal with the problem. Dealing with the problem seems to come to trying to reason with the methodist and skeptic about their positions. Dealing with the problem of the criterion seems to come to providing a means to resolve this dispute between the particularist, methodist, and skeptic.

This insight—that the problem of the criterion is a metaepistemological problem—also uncovers a confusion in Chisholm's rejection of skepticism. Earlier we noted that Chisholm never offers any reasons why he finds the skeptic's position unacceptable, except to claim that his approach has one thing in favor of it that the others do not—"the fact that we *do* know many things, after all."[49] It is clear now that our skeptic need not deny that we know many things in order to maintain her thesis that answering (A) and (B) is impossible.[50]

Could this problem be the same as Sextus's problem of the criterion? They are certainly closely related, but I believe that they are also different from one another. The difference lies in the presuppositions involved in the posing of each problem. This is where the context of inquiry becomes important. One difference concerns Sextus's skepticism. It is not a dogmatic skepticism. Sextus only claims that *it appears to him* that the dispute between those who claim some impression true or false and those who disagree cannot be resolved. Sextus makes no dogmatic claims and takes no *position*. Chisholm's skeptic is quite dogmatic—you *cannot* answer (A) until you answer (B) and you *cannot* answer (B) until you answer (A).

Furthermore, Sextus presupposes Stoic epistemology, and Chisholm does not.[51] For example, suppose there are two individuals, S and S'. S claims that some proposition h is true and S' claims that h is false. Sextus does not dispute the epistemological issue, that is, what is required for S or S' to pass judgment on h. The Stoics supply the epistemology. "Firm assent" to h is required in order for S to know h. Firm assent is a criterion of truth for the Stoics. Sextus raised doubts about the criterion, and in doing so, argued that it *seemed to him* that disputes over claims to know h are incapable of settlement. To settle the dispute, one would need a criterion (C) that was the product of a proof of its truth that was confirmed by an already established criterion, and so on. Chisholm, on the other hand, comes with his own epistemology—particularism. He claims that in order to pass judgment on h, we do not need any test or criterion. And that we can only "deal" with disputes on this issue by begging the question.

Because the presuppositions in each case are different, the problems are different problems. But they are closely related because if one could "settle" Sextus's problem, one could also, it seems to me, settle Chisholm's problem. Rescher's explanation of the problem seems to be the same as Chisholm's, for he too interprets the skeptic dogmatically and does not presuppose Stoic epistemology. So we seem to have two different versions of the problem of the criterion, an ancient one and a modern one. In the following chapters, I will offer my resolution of these problems as well as my analysis of what problems we are left to answer.

NOTES

Parts of this chapter are reprinted, with changes, from two earlier papers—"Roderick Chisholm and the Problem of the Criterion" and "Reply to Chisholm on the Problem of the Criterion," *Philosophical Papers* 17, no. 3 (Nov. 1988): 217–29, 235–36, with permission of the editor of *Philosophical Papers*.

    1. Roderick M. Chisholm, *Perceiving: A Philosophical Study* (Ithaca, N. Y.: Cornell University Press, 1957); *Theory of Knowledge,* hereafter referred to as *TK*; and *Foundations of Knowing,* hereafter referred to as *FK*.

    2. Roderick M. Chisholm, *The Problem of the Criterion* (Milwaukee, Wis.: Marquette University Press, 1973).

    3. Chisholm, *FK*, 61.

90 *Chapter Four*

4. Chisholm's basic position on the problem of the criterion has not changed with the publication of the third edition of *TK* (1989).

5. Chisholm, *FK*, 62.

6. Ibid., 63; cited from Mercier, *Critèriologie*, 234.

7. Chisholm, *FK*, 64.

8. Chisholm also cites P. Coffey's *Epistemology or Theory of Knowledge* in this regard. Coffey cites Descartes's reply to the seventh set of objections in his discussion of the problem of the criterion.

9. Coffey, 127.

10. *The Philosophical Works of Descartes*, vol. 2, tr. by E. Haldane and G. R. T. Ross (Cambridge: Cambridge University Press, 1967), 282.

11. Coffey, 127.

12. Chisholm, *FK*, 64–65.

13. Ibid., 65.

14. Ibid., 66.

15. Chisholm's account of the skeptic's position is quite different from Sextus's account. Sextus "has a view" (undogmatically), which is not one of Chisholm's three possible views, unless one *misconstrues* Sextus's skepticism as a variety of dogmatic skepticism. Furthermore, if my analysis of Montaigne's "position" is correct (i.e., the same as Sextus's), then Montaigne would not be one of Chisholm's skeptics either. I will discuss similarities and differences between Sextus and Chisholm at the end of this chapter.

16. Chisholm, *FK*, 75.

17. Ibid., 67.

18. Ibid.

19. Ibid.

20. Ibid.

21. Ibid. This criterion is intentionally left vague by Chisholm because a detailed formulation is unimportant for his discussion. He states: "Just what these relations to our sensations might be is a matter we may leave open, for our present purposes."

22. Ibid., 69.

23. Ibid., 67.

24. Ibid.

25. Ibid.

26. Ibid.

27. Ibid.

28. Ibid.

29. See Richard Feldman, "Fallibilism and Knowing That One Knows," *Philosophical Review* 90 (1981): 266–82.

30. Chisholm reaffirms his commitment to this thesis in the third edition of *Theory of Knowledge*, 99–100.

31. Chisholm, *FK*, 69.

32. Ibid., 75.

33. Chisholm, *Perceiving*, 38.

34. Chisholm, *FK*, 75.
35. Ibid.
36. Chisholm, *Perceiving*, 38.
37. Apparently the element of arbitrariness in the *skeptic's* position is in maintaining or presupposing the condition that in order for knowledge to be possible of either particulars or criteria, we must first have knowledge of the other. Chisholm never explicitly states what it is about the skeptic's position that he takes to be arbitrary.
38. Roderick Chisholm, "Reply to Amico on the Problem of the Criterion," *Philosophical Papers* 17, no. 3 (Nov. 1988): 231.
39. Ibid., 234.
40. Ibid.
41. Ibid., 232.
42. Ibid.
43. Ibid.
44. Ibid.
45. Montaigne took himself to be discussing the same problem as Sextus Empiricus, but we have determined in Chapter 2 that while their accounts are similar, it is very likely that some of their presuppositions were different, and, hence, they are not discussing the exact same problem.
46. I refer to the presuppositions of Sextus here loosely, because strictly speaking Sextus would say that he makes no presuppositions himself about what *is*.
47. Sosa, "Foundations of Foundationalism," 558.
48. Chisholm, *FK*, 75.
49. Ibid.
50. Thanks to Richard Feldman for pointing this out to me.
51. We have been using the term "presuppose" in Stalnaker's sense to mean pragmatically presuppose. (See "Pragmatic Presuppositions.") This does not fit well with Sextus's Pyrrhonian skepticism because it requires one to take the *truth* of a proposition for granted. Sextus never takes the truth of any proposition for granted. However, it would not be mistaken to say that Sextus does "assume for the sake of argument" the Stoic position, and then try to show how it involves some contradiction. In this sense I think it is fair to say that Sextus presupposes Stoic epistemology in his "wheel argument."

This judgment also fits well with my characterization of pragmatic presupposition in Chapter 1, because Stoic epistemology certainly seems to form part of the framework for what counts as an acceptable answer to his question.

Chapter 5

Problems and Solutions

FOUNDATIONALISM VS. NONFOUNDATIONALISM

Chisholm makes two claims worth further consideration. The first is that *any attempt* to solve the problem begs the question. The second is that there are *only three* possible approaches to the problem of the criterion. I shall begin with the latter claim. One way to approach this issue, which seems fruitful, is to consider Chisholm's portrayal of the problem in the light of the debate between foundationalist and nonfoundationalist theories of justification in epistemology. This is the approach of Ernest Sosa and my outline will follow his analysis[1].

The debate between foundationalists and nonfoundationalists (mainly coherentists) centers around the *infinite regress* argument. Generally speaking, foundationalists argue that if our beliefs are not founded on or justified by some epistemically privileged beliefs—ones that either need no justification or are self-justifying or evident—then justification will either proceed in a vicious circle (which is no justification at all) or to an infinite regress (which is impossible). Coherentists, on the other hand, argue that the justification of our beliefs consists in their being a part of a mutually supportive set of beliefs. Sosa comments, "Contemporary epistemology must choose between the solid security of the ancient foundationalist pyramid and the risky adventure of the new coherentist raft."[2]

Yet foundationalists and coherentists share certain assumptions as well, and these can best be explained by drawing a few distinctions. The first is between formal foundationalism and substantive foundationalism. Formal foundationalism (FF) is the thesis that a definition of epistemic justification can be given recursively in terms of a nonepistemic basis property and a nonepistemic generator. For example, a justified belief could be defined in terms of a nonepistemic basis property (e.g., indubitability) and a nonepistemic generating relation (e.g., deduction) such that the class of beliefs that are either indubitable (has the basis property) or can be generated (is deducible) from beliefs with such a basis property are the class of justified beliefs. Hence, (FF) entails a doctrine of supervenience. Epistemic terms supervene on the nonepistemic. As Sosa explains:

> For an evaluative property Φ, for every x, if x has Φ then there is a non-evaluative property (perhaps a relational property) Ψ such that (i) x has Ψ and (ii) necessarily, whatever has Ψ has Φ.[3]

The denial of the doctrine of supervenience can be called the doctrine of the autonomy of Φ—the thesis that evaluative properties can be exemplified notwithstanding the fact that they do not supervene on nonevaluative properties. Sosa calls the denial of (FF) "pessimism."

The coherence theory (at least the standard forms of it), then, is a form of (FF) because it defines justified belief in terms of a basis property—coherence within a set of beliefs—and a generating relation, such as deduction. Coherentism is not opposed to (FF). Rather, coherentism is opposed to substantive foundationalism (also known as radical foundationalism), which maintains that coherence *never* serves as a basis property. One might, then, call radical coherentism the position that coherence alone can serve as the basis. There are many possible intermediary positions between radical coherentism and radical foundationalism. For example, modest foundationalism is a form of substantive foundationalism, which, in all cases, I believe, denies that coherence is the only basis (radical coherentism). However, in most versions, it embraces coherence as a partial basis, while, I suppose, other versions could deny that coherence is any basis of justification. All such positions are forms of (FF). The following illustration may help to clarify these distinctions (Fig. 5–1):

Our second distinction divides substantive foundationalism into epistemic foundationalism (EF) and metaepistemic foundationalism (MEF). Epistemic foundationalism concerns the justification of beliefs about the nonepistemic, about the justification of beliefs that are not themselves about justification. Metaepistemic foundationalism concerns the justification of beliefs about the epistemic. Hence, (EF) maintains that there must be foundational beliefs, that is, beliefs that do not receive all of their justification from coherence with other beliefs, but rather get at least some of their justification from some factor independent of a person's system of beliefs. (MEF) makes the same claim at the metalevel about epistemic beliefs, beliefs about epistemic justification.

In the chapter 4, we learned that the problem of the criterion is a metaepistemological problem. It concerns whether we can give an epistemic justification of epistemic claims. Are particularism and methodism, then, epistemological or metaepistemological positions? Sosa thinks they are metaepistemological.

Formal Foundationalism → (Logically Entails) **Doctrine of Supervenience**
A definition of epistemic justification can be given in terms of a nonepistemic basis property and a nonepistemic generator.

For an evaluative property Φ, for every x, if x has Φ then there is a nonevaluative property Ψ such that (i) x has Ψ and (ii) necessarily, whatever has Ψ has Φ.

↑
↑
(is a form of)

Radical Coherentism
Coherence is the only basis for justification of the nonepistemic.

↖ ↖ ↖
(is a form of)

Substantive Foundationalism   **Skepticism**

↙   ↘
either   or

Coherence is not the only basis;   Coherence is never the basis.
Most forms of modest Foundationalism   (Radical foundationalism)
                    Some possible forms of modest
                    foundationalism.

Particularism and methodism are meta-epistemological positions, for they tell us which justifies which of two sorts of *epistemic* knowledge. They tell us whether our knowledge of certain epistemic principles is based on our knowledge that we have bits of knowledge of a certain related kind (e.g., of the external world, that I have two hands), or whether, conversely, our knowledge that we have bits of knowledge of a particular kind rests on our knowledge of certain related epistemic principles.[4]

Actually, parts of particularism and methodism are theses that exist on both levels.[5] On the epistemological level, particularism tells us that we know or are justified in believing, for example, that I have a left hand. It might explain such knowledge or justification of the nonepistemic in terms of self-presenting states or that which is evident to me. A methodist might claim that I know or am justified in believing any proposition derived from a reliable belief-forming process or which I clearly and distinctly perceive.

There are a number of possible positions at this epistemological level. Here are a few of the more obvious permutations.

- *Particularism*: I know certain particulars, such as, that I have a left hand. Such particular knowledge is possible without knowing and/or applying any criterion or method, and this enables me to fashion the criteria of knowledge.
- *Methodism*: I know any proposition that I clearly and distinctly perceive. Such knowledge is possible without knowing and/or generalizing from particular instances of knowledge, and this enables me to identify particular cases of knowledge.
- *Skepticism 1*: Knowledge of particulars is dependent upon prior knowledge of criteria. Knowledge of criteria is dependent upon prior knowledge of particulars. Therefore, knowledge of either is impossible.
- *Skepticism 2*: Knowledge of particulars requires indubitability. Such knowledge would allow me to list what I know, but there are no such indubitable propositions.
- *Particular Intuitionism*: I know certain particulars, such as, that I have a left hand. Such particular knowledge is possible without knowing and/or applying any criterion or method, but this does not enable me to fashion a criterion of knowledge.
- *Methodological Intuitionism*: I know any proposition that I clearly and distinctly perceive. Such knowledge is possible without knowing and/or generalizing from particular instances of knowledge, but this does not enable me to identify particular cases of knowledge.
- *Relational Skeptic*: Even if I had knowledge of particulars, I could not thereby fashion a correct criterion of knowledge; and even if I knew the cor-

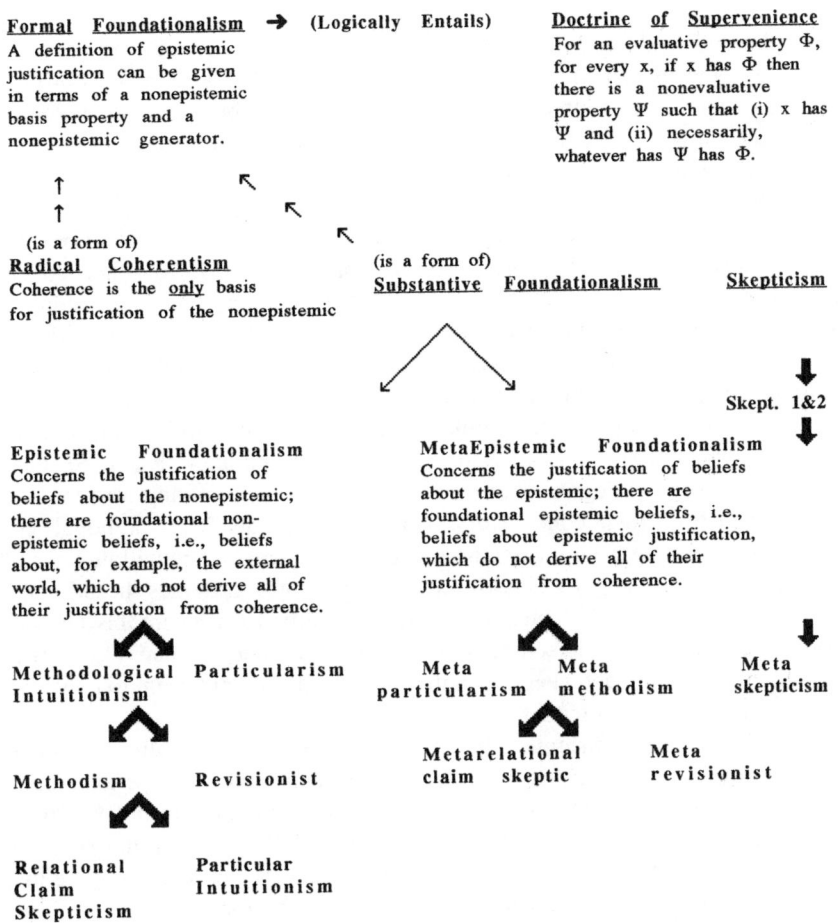

Figure 5-2. *Epistemic Map 2*

rect criterion of knowledge, I could not use it to pick out particular instances of knowledge.
- *Revisionist*: I know a few particulars and part of the correct criterion, and from this knowledge, I can fill in the rest of both.
- *Revisionist Skeptic*: I know a few particulars and part of the correct criterion, but from this knowledge, I cannot fill in the rest of both.

All of these positions concern justification of beliefs about the nonepistemic. These positions can be added to our original illustration and provide a picture of how they are all related (Fig. 5-2).

It is interesting to notice that coherentism is not among these alternatives.

Yet coherentism does concern the justification of beliefs about the nonepistemic; for instance, I know any proposition that coheres with my body of beliefs. Why is coherentism not listed as a form of methodism? There are straightforward reasons for this that can be explained in terms of two concepts, epistemic priority and epistemic dependence.

According to Roderick Firth, the thesis of epistemic priority maintains that "some statements have some degree of warrant which is independent of (and in this sense 'prior to') the warrant (if any) that they derive from their coherence with other statements."[6] In terms of the positions listed, all seem to accept and presuppose this principle of epistemic priority except Skepticism 1 and Skepticism 2. This is so because they are all forms of substantive foundationalism (SF) and (SF) presupposes this principle of epistemic priority. Particularism, methodism, revisionism, methodological intuitionism, particular intuitionism, and relational claim skepticism all maintain that some statements have some of degree of warrant that is independent of any warrant they may derive from their coherence with other statements. Thus, although coherentism does begin with a method or criterion—coherence within a set of beliefs—it is not categorized with methodism because it denies the principle of epistemic priority. Noncoherentist forms of methodism accept the thesis of epistemic priority. In this sense, coherentism is another alternative to particularism, methodism, and skepticism that Chisholm does not seem to consider. I will return to this matter shortly.

By "the thesis of epistemic dependence," I mean the following: If knowledge of proposition P (or justified belief in P) is epistemically dependent upon another proposition Q, then knowledge of P (or justified belief in P) requires prior knowledge of Q (or justified belief in Q).[7] If we substitute types of beliefs for individual beliefs—for example, particulars and methods—we find many of the positions listed above subscribing to one form or another of this thesis. The particularist claims that methods are epistemically dependent upon particulars; methodists have it the other way around, and Skepticism 1 has it both ways. Coherentism, however, denies the thesis of epistemic dependence. A coherentist might argue that either knowledge of (or justification of) particulars and methods occurs simultaneously or that temporal priority is irrelevant to their conception of knowledge (or justification). The relevant concept is membership in the appropriate set of beliefs. This denial of the thesis of epistemic dependence for particulars and methods sets coherentism apart from all of the other positions we have considered (i.e., all the other approaches to the problem of the criterion).

At this epistemic level, however, none of these positions is an "approach" to the problem of the criterion, because that is a metaepistemological problem. It concerns the justification of certain *epistemic* claims. Of course, as

Figures 5–1 and 5–2 indicate, there are as many counterpart positions at the meta-level under the heading of metaepistemic foundationalism. There is also a metaepistemic coherentism which would be a form of metaepistemic non-foundationalism (MENF). (MENF) maintains that there are no foundational epistemic beliefs and that beliefs about the epistemic derive all of their justification from coherence or some other relation to other beliefs of the subject.

At the metalevel, is coherentism an approach that Chisholm neglected to consider? Does its rejection of the principle of epistemic priority and the principle of epistemic dependence make it significantly different from other forms of methodism? We discovered that Rescher's attempt to meet and overcome the problem of the criterion involved an attempt to formulate a system of justification that is significantly different from coherentism. Rescher took coherentism to be inadequate to deal with the problem. Perhaps a closer look at coherentism is warranted at this time.

One way that a coherentist might argue that plays on her rejection of the principles of epistemic priority and epistemic dependence is as follows. Consider the following propositions based on Chisholm's two pairs of questions (A) and (B):

1. In order to answer (A), one must already possess the answer to (B), so that (B) can be used in the justification of (A).
2. In order to answer (B), one must already possess the answer to (A), so that (A) can be used in the justification of (B).
3. One can answer (A) and one can answer (B).
4. Propositions (1), (2), and (3) are mutually inconsistent.[8]

The particularist, methodist, and skeptic all have one thing in common, they accept 4 because they are all committed to some form of the principle of epistemic dependence. The methodist accepts 3 and 1 and rejects 2. The particularist accepts 3 and 2 and rejects 1. The skeptic accepts 1 and 2 and rejects 3.

The coherentist, however, sees another way out. There are two ways to interpret her alternative. If we interpret "already" in 1 and 2 in some nontemporal, nonlogical way, then she could simply reject proposition 4. She could then claim that there is no logical inconsistency between 1, 2 and 3 unless one also assumes another proposition—the principle of epistemic priority—and she denies this. The other way to interpret her alternative is that she denies *both* 1 and 2 *because* she denies the principle of epistemic priority, which is implicit in 1 and 2. Does the skeptic accept this principle? Earlier, I claimed that the skeptic denies this principle, but a skeptic could accept it conditionally by accepting that the principle of epistemic priority is a necessary condition for knowledge or justified belief, but there are no beliefs with such warrant. There are many ways to be a skeptic.

Paul Moser uses a similar strategy in *Knowledge and Evidence* to provide what he calls a noncircular solution to the problem of the criterion.[9] His approach is to offer a metajustification of his epistemic theory—explanatory particularism—via the method of reflective equilibrium. Reflective equilibrium is the term coined by John Rawls for a mode of justification first introduced by Nelson Goodman. Concerning the justification of deduction, Goodman claims:

> [D]eductive inferences are justified by their conformity to valid general rules, and . . . general rules are justified by their conformity to valid inferences. But this circle is a virtuous one. The point is that rules and particular inferences alike are justified by being brought into agreement with each other. *A rule is amended if it yields an inference we are unwilling to accept; an inference is rejected if it violates a rule we are unwilling to amend.* The process of justification is a delicate one of making mutual adjustments between rules and accepted inferences; and in the agreement achieved lies the only justification needed for either.[10]

For Moser, we explain particular epistemic intuitions about justification by epistemic principles and vice versa. Our goal is "maximal explanatory power." Both principles and particular intuitions are revisable, which makes his account, so Moser claims, superior to standard versions of both particularism and methodism. This is so because it avoids begging the question against the skeptic. He also avers that his explanatory particularism avoids the problem of vicious circularity because it denies that "we can justify our epistemic principles solely by what those principles countenance as knowledge or justification."[11] It provides him with what he takes to be a noncircular solution to the problem of the criterion.

Moser's approach is a form of coherentism at the metalevel. His thesis would deny the principle of epistemic priority at the metalevel since both particulars and principles are revisable. This would make reflective equilibrium a form of weak coherentism in that it maintains that justification is wholly a matter of relations among beliefs, but denies that, as Haack explains it, "no belief is more secure than any other."[12] However all beliefs are revisable. As Michael Williams explains it, there are three reasons for considering reflective equilibrium a coherence method: (1) the resulting beliefs need not be all of one type; some may be particulars and some principles; (2) different people's resulting beliefs need not be the same or even consistent with one another; and (3) the resulting beliefs are always *revisable*; they are not given a privileged status.[13]

Is this approach different enough from methodism to qualify as another approach to the problem of the criterion that Chisholm failed to consider? I think not and perhaps this explains why Chisholm does not discuss it separately. My reason is as follows. The fact that coherentism denies the principle of epistemic priority and the principle of epistemic dependence, does not make it any less a form of methodism. Coherence is a criterion or method by means of which coherentists claim to determine what constitutes knowledge or justified belief. Hence, they are faced with the same question as other methodists: how do you know that coherence or reflective equilibrium is a good method for sorting out good beliefs from bad ones? This method, like any other, needs justification. It seems that either you already need to know which beliefs are good and which beliefs are bad in order to test your method or criterion by its fidelity to this knowledge, or you need a meta-metacriterion that picks out this metacriterion as the correct metacriterion, and so on.

And so we are back on the wheel or off on an infinite regress! This means that Moser does not solve the problem of the criterion. Indeed, if we recall Rescher's discussion in Chapter 3, methodological pragmatism can be understood as a form of coherentism or even reflective equilibrium, which Rescher himself concedes does not *solve* the problem of the criterion. He claims that a solution is impossible, but that his approach comes as close as one can come to a justification. I believe that this is the most that Moser can claim to have achieved.[14]

Some have argued that although any attempt to solve the problem of the criterion will result in circularity, the coherence theory can be justified via coherence, and hence justified circularly, but such justification is not *viciously* circular.[15] This line of reasoning is inspired by F. H. Bradley who claimed:

> For if you think at all so as to discriminate between truth and falsehood, you will find that you cannot accept open self-contradiction. Hence to think is to judge, and to judge is to criticize, and to criticize is to use a criterion of reality. And surely to doubt this would be mere blindness or confused self-deception. But, if so, it is clear that, in rejecting the inconsistent as appearance, we are applying a positive knowledge of the ultimate nature of things. Ultimate reality is such that it does not contradict itself; here is an *absolute criterion. And it is proved absolute by the fact that, either in endeavoring to deny it, or even in attempting to doubt it, we tacitly assume its validity*.[16]

Bradley seems to be saying that because we *cannot avoid* depending upon coherence, *whatever* our criterion might be, such circularity is not question begging because coherence is not *arbitrarily* chosen, but rather is *unavoidably* chosen.[17] Two points can be made about Bradley's thesis. The first concerns vicious circularity and the second concerns the laws of logic. Let me begin with vicious circularity.

What makes an argument viciously circular? Standard cases of vicious circularity involve premise circularity, where the conclusion of an argument is literally stated as a premise. Precisely what makes such arguments vicious? Well, it seems to me that the point of an argument is to rationally move someone toward or persuade someone to accept the conclusion on the basis of the premises. If the conclusion is literally stated as a premise, then one cannot be moved to accept the conclusion on the basis of the premises, because one has already accepted it in asserting the premises. Circular arguments, then, cannot be persuasive.[18]

Bradley's argument is not premise circular but, nonetheless, I believe that its circularity is just as vicious. It involves a kind of rule circularity. Salmon characterizes rule circularity thus: "An argument can be circular . . . by exhibiting a form whose validity is asserted by the very conclusion that is to be proved."[19] The idea behind rule circularity is that a rule or principle is established as valid by an argument that employs the very rule or principle in question to do the establishing. What makes such arguments vicious is that, again, one cannot be rationally moved to accept the conclusion (the rule or principle) if one must accept this rule or principle and employ it to establish the conclusion. It cannot be persuasive. One must accept the conclusion to establish it.

Bradley's argument is rule circular in this way because he must employ coherence in order to establish coherence as the correct criterion. But isn't Bradley's point that we cannot help but employ coherence, and hence the viciousness is somehow mitigated? This brings me to the second point about the laws of logic. I would argue along with C. D. Broad, Nicholas Rescher, and Bertrand Russell[20] that what coherence depends upon in this argument is the acceptance of certain logical principles, which, although part of Bradley's coherent system, must be justified independent of the system. The principles of logic provide, as Russell claims, "the skeleton or framework within which the test of coherence applies, and they themselves cannot be established by this test."[21] If the laws of logic form the basis for coherence, as I believe they do, then Bradley is incorrect in his claim that we can't help but employ coherence.

Russell claimed that "[I]f the law of contradiction itself were subjected to the test of coherence, we should find that, if we choose to suppose it false, nothing will any longer be incoherent with anything else."[22] Robert Lehe claims that Russell is wrong here, that if we suppose the principle of contradiction false, "nothing would follow from this position, since there would be no principle by which anything could follow."[23] He argues that the principle of contradiction relies on coherence instead of having it the other way around. But I think this is wrong because if one were to suppose the law of contradiction to be false—that a proposition and its negation could both be true at the same time and in the same respect—then *nothing* would any longer be incoherent. Coherence presupposes the law of contradiction, because for beliefs or propositions to cohere, they must satisfy this law, not the other way around. It seems to me that coherence only makes sense under this logical presupposition.[24] And so, it seems that such a defense of coherence fails as a solution to the problem of the criterion because it is viciously circular.

Broadly speaking, then, although we have found that there are other alternatives to the three that Chisholm discusses, for the purposes of a discussion of approaches to the problem of the criterion, they are simply variations on these three themes. This includes various forms of coherentism, reflective equilibrium, modest foundationalism, and "foundherentism."[25]

In answering this first claim made by Chisholm, we have focused our attention on some of the presuppositions of particularists, methodists, and skeptics. This is a strategy that will be of great importance in Chapter 6 when I attempt to discredit the skeptical position.

THE INFINITE REGRESS

Concerning Chisholm's second claim that *any* attempt to solve the problem of the criterion begs the question, some have argued that an infinite regress of justification is another alternative to solve the problem, and not all infinite regresses are unacceptable. If this is true, then Chisholm's claim would be false and we would have found another approach to the problem.

Traditionally, the infinite regress has been considered an unacceptable mode of justification. Aristotle discusses the infinite regress in his *Posterior Analytics*:

> The first school, assuming there is no way of knowing other than by demonstration, maintains that an infinite regress is involved, on the ground that if behind the prior stands no primary, we could not know the posterior through the prior (wherein *they are right, for one cannot traverse an infinite series*).[26]

The regress argument is often made as a means of persuading others to adopt some form of foundationalism. Chisholm argues that often we reply to a query about what justifies us in believing some proposition, by citing some other proposition that justifies it. And when asked what justifies us in believing this second proposition, we cite a third proposition that justifies it. He then claims:

> We might try to continue *ad infinitum,* justifying each new claim that we elicit by still another claim. Or we might be tempted to complete a vicious circle. . . . But if we are rational beings we will do neither of these things. For we shall find, that our Socratic questions lead us to a proper stopping place.[27]

But why is an infinite regress of justification unacceptable? Chisholm offers no argument, and probably thinks the reasons are obvious. There have been many arguments against the infinite regress and if any of them are sound, we need not continue this inquiry.[28] But there have also been many arguments presented supporting various kinds of infinite regresses of justification,.[29] and if any have merit, we should explore this issue further. Jay Harker offers a good survey of six types of arguments against the regress and explains why each fails.[30] I will only examine his last argument here because it, more than the others, leaves open the possibility of an infinite regress of justification.

Harker's sixth argument type involves a claim make by Pollock that if there is an infinite regress of justification, then justification is detached from reality. An argument against the infinite regress follows from two assumptions: (1) that there must be some connection between justification and truth; justification must be "truthconducive,"[31] and (2) if an infinite chain of justification is possible, then it must be possible for a system of beliefs to have all of its justified beliefs justified solely by their relationships to other justified beliefs.

The argument against the regress then runs as follows. If (2) is true, then beliefs are justified independent of any relation they might bear to reality—to the world. But if (1) is true, then justification must have some relation to reality—to the way the world is. Assumption (2) implies that (1) is false, that is, if there is an infinite regress of justification, then justification is completely detached from reality.

Harker claims that (1) is incontestable but that (2) is false. He employs a distinction made by Alston between a *mediately justified belief* and an *immediately justified belief*:

> A *mediately justified belief* is any belief that is justified by virtue of standing in some relationship to some other belief(s).
>
> An *immediately justified belief* is any belief that is justified by something other than any relationship it bears to any other belief(s).[32]

But a belief can be justified both ways, partly mediately and partly immediately. Surely, if it is possible to have an infinite chain of justification, it is possible to have such a chain where some beliefs are both mediately and immediately justified. Hence, if an infinite chain of justification is possible, then (2) is false.

The consequent of proposition (2) embodies the thesis of radical coherentism, that coherence (mediate justification) is the only basis for justification. It denies the principle of epistemic priority. Hence, one conditional conclusion that follows is that if radical coherentism is true, then an infinite chain of justification is impossible. It would be impossible because such an infinite chain would be completely detached from the world and would thus be no real justification.

If this line of reasoning is correct, then *some* kinds of infinite chains of justification have been ruled out, but others have not. Anyone who endorses the principle of epistemic priority to some degree could consistently endorse an infinite regress of justification. This would include foundationalists of every ilk and more moderate coherentists—anyone who would allow that some beliefs derive some of their justification from some way other than the relationships they bear to other beliefs. Chisholm is certainly in this category, and an infinite chain of justification is not an option he considers. Could it be a nonquestion-begging way to solve the problem of the criterion?

One suggestion for infinite regresses of justification is that what is required for the justification of a belief is that it be justifiable by reference to its successor. Bruce Aune suggests that as long as we can produce the successor upon demand, we need not proceed along the chain any further than is requested.[33] Sosa offers an example of the kind of linking relation that would produce such an infinite regress of justification:

(J1) P justifies (would justify) Q iff that P is justified is sufficient for Q to be justified.

An infinite regress is then generated in accordance with (J1) as follows:

(P1) that there is at least one real number in the interval <0–1>.
(P2) that there are at least two real numbers in the interval <0–1>.
(P3) ... etc.
(P2) justifies (P1), (P3) justifies (P2), etc., *ad infinitum*.[34]

By similar reasoning one could imagine the following infinite sequence:

(J1) P justifies Q iff that P is justified is sufficient for Q to be justified.

Regress example:
    (C1) Criterion of Truth
    (P1) Proof of Criterion (C1)
    (C2) Criterion of Truth*
    (P2) Proof of Criterion (C2)
    (C3) ... etc.
    (P1) justifies (C1), (C2) justifies (P1), (P2) justifies (C2), *ad infinitum*.

Is this kind of a justification possible and could it solve the problem of the criterion? It does seem that this kind of justification is possible, but such a justification will not solve the problem of the criterion. A solution to the problem of the criterion, ancient or modern, requires settling a dispute. Settling a dispute requires that one somehow *show* or *justify*, in a nonquestion-begging way, one's position—particularism, methodism, or skepticism. And if one's belief is justified by some infinite justificatory chain, it cannot be *demonstrably shown* to be justified.[35]

Furthermore, there is the additional problem that it is quite possible to have two different infinite justificatory chains each justifying a different position or proposition, and hence equally justifiable. How would we decide between them? To solve the problem of the criterion, we would have to decide between them in a nonarbitrary, nonquestion-begging way. So now it seems that we can add this point as another reason why an infinite regress of justification cannot solve the problem.

DISSOLUTIONS OF THE PROBLEMS OF THE CRITERION

If an infinite regress of justification cannot solve the problem of the criterion, and if there are only three possible general approaches to the problem as Chisholm claims, and they all beg the question, then how can the problem, ancient or modern, be solved? In Chapter 1, I made a distinction between solutions, dissolutions, resolutions, and repudiations of problems. A solution is a positive answer to the problem posed by a question, which removes rational doubt. A dissolution is an answer that shows the impossibility of solving the problem and thereby removes any rational doubt about how to answer the question that heretofore had posed a problem. It is a dissolution because where one may have thought the question posed a problem (i.e., where one may have had rational doubt about how to answer the question), one is led to see that there is no rational doubt about how to answer the question. In effect, the problem is shown to be a pseudoproblem. It is a question for which one no longer has any rational doubt. A resolution is either a solution or a dissolution, and a repudiation is a denial of the presupposition made by the person posing the problem. This is a way of denying the basis upon which rational doubt is founded.[36] In what is to follow, I will offer a dissolution of both the ancient problem and the modern problem. In Chapter 6, I will repudiate the modern problem.

The Ancient Problem

The ancient problem of the criterion characterized by Sextus Empiricus can be formulated thus: How can one settle the dispute between individuals who claim certain impressions true or false and those who disagree? Sextus's answer is that since the claims appear equipollent to him, he cannot settle the dispute. In such a dispute, Sextus suspends judgment.

We should understand Sextus's argument within the context of a dialogue with the Stoics. The Stoics had claimed that they could discern the true from the false whenever they had "firm assent"; and firm assent required irrefutable provability. Since it appears, Sextus argued, that no claim can meet this standard of irrefutable provability, and only meeting such a standard could settle a dispute between individuals who disagree about some claim, it appears that he cannot settle the dispute and should suspend judgment. Sextus never concludes that knowledge is impossible, and his "wheel argument," as it has come to be called, makes no dogmatic assertions or claims to truth. His argument merely reflects how conflicting claims *appear to him*; it merely reflects his "view." He never claims that settling the dispute is impossible. Even if he is correct in *his* assessment, his argument expresses *no position*, but rather, it reflects only his impression or view.

It is difficult for me, then, to see the force of his argument. Rescher, Chisholm, Moser, and most other authors with whom I am familiar seem to have missed this point and misinterpreted Sextus's argument as presenting *a position*, like a dogmatic skeptic, and Sextus strongly and repeatedly denies all dogmatism. But if we take his protestations seriously and conclude that Sextus maintains no position, that his argument does no more than express Sextus's impressions at that moment, then his argument seems of little philosophical significance. Of course, one might argue that the implication of his argument is that *any* rational person would agree with Sextus's claims of equipollence when confronted with the same dispute. But Sextus never asserts this either.

It is a mistake to take Sextus's argument out of its Stoic context and portray it as making the dogmatic claim that it is impossible to validate a criterion of truth. Rescher does precisely this in *Methodological Pragmatism* by saying, "It is in principle impossible to make a direct check of this sort on the functioning of our truth-determining methods."[37] But in fact, Sextus's argument establishes very little—only what his impressions are at that time about settling the dispute.

One question that arises from these considerations concerns the Stoic standard of irrefutable provability. Whatever force Sextus's argument has rests upon this Stoic standard. Is it a necessary condition for settling a dispute about the truth of impressions? Could it be a sufficient condition, but not a necessary one? Perhaps other standards would be sufficient as well. We could formulate this question more generally as: *What* is required to settle a dispute about truth or knowledge claims?

Recall the beginning of Sextus's argument:

1. [SHOW] Disagreement between those who judge impressions . . . is incapable of settlement.
2. A person who judges one impression true and another false does so either critically and with a proof or uncritically and without proof.
3. But a person can judge the impression in neither way because:
   a. If a person judges uncritically and without proof, then his or her opponent simply disagrees with his or her claim and no settlement has been achieved (he/she will be discredited).
   b. If a person judges critically, then he/she must do so by a criterion of truth.

The reason premise 2 states that "a person who judges one impression true and another false does so either critically and with a proof or uncritically and without proof," is because the Stoic standard of irrefutable provability is being presupposed as the only standard that can settle the dispute. Therefore, if a judgment is made critically it *must* be done with a *proof*. As we discovered in Chapter 2, the Stoics changed their original position to try to accommodate objections raised by the skeptics. Originally, they maintained that *having* a cognitive impression is criterial of truth. A cognitive impression guaranteed its own truthfulness. When challenged by the Skeptics on how they could be sure that any particular cognitive impression was indeed cognitive, the Stoics changed their position by adding a condition to these cognitive impressions that there be "no obstacle" to the impression. As I discussed earlier, this change led to the demise of the Stoic position by introducing the possibility of error.

It seems to me that they never should have made this change. They should have simply replied that when someone is having a genuine cognitive impression, simply the *having* of such an impression guarantees its truth; "it lays hold of us, almost by the very hairs, as they say, and drags us off to assent, needing nothing else to help it be thus impressive or to suggest its superiority over all others."[38] Had the Stoics maintained their original position and the Skeptics disputed the claim that there are any such cognitive impressions by asking for *further justification* of their position by means of a proof, then the Stoics could have questioned either (1) whether any further justification is necessary, or (2) whether a proof is the only acceptable means of justification. As Max Black points out in his discussion on the nature of justification:

> A demand for justification is normally taken to imply a *discrepancy with some acceptable standard*. And a satisfactory justification is one which neutralizes the apparent discrepancy by showing it to be consistent with, or deducible from, the relevant standard.[39]

If the Stoic and the Skeptic cannot agree about the standard of justification, then it seems to make the Skeptic's demand for a justification (by a mutually accepted standard) fruitless because he has none. If Black is correct, then one condition necessary for settling a dispute would be agreement based upon a mutually accepted standard by which disputed claims are adjudicated. The Stoics, then, might have claimed that while an irrefutable proof is sufficient to settle the dispute, it is not a necessary condition. They might have claimed that having a cognitive impression is sufficient for its justification, and that an irrefutable proof is impossible to provide anyhow. If Sextus disagreed here, they would be involved in a *different* discussion about what conditions are necessary for settling a dispute. So it seems that the course of their argument would have taken a different turn if the Stoics had not changed their original position.

Since Sextus never maintained a position concerning the problem of the criterion or the presuppositions involved in posing the problem, the standard of irrefutable provability is no part of his position. His strategy is to show, assuming the Stoic's background assumptions and methodology *for the sake of the argument*, that it seems to him that his opponent's position either involves a contradiction or there is an argument that contradicts his position, which can be generated from his position. It also seemed to Sextus that his opponent could not successfully argue against this contradicting position.

In the light of Sextus's skepticism—of not taking any position—it seems clear that if the Stoics had maintained their original position, the problem of the criterion as Sextus characterized it would not have arisen at that time. Rather than ask: "*How* do you settle a dispute between individuals who claim certain impressions true or false and those who disagree?"—where it is presupposed that settling a dispute requires irrefutable provability—Sextus would be asking: "*What* standard is required to settle a dispute about conflicting claims to truth?" The latter question inquires about the standard for satisfactory epistemic metajustification, while the former presupposes a particular Stoic standard and inquires how one can settle a dispute *given* this standard.

It seems to me that Sextus's characterization of the problem of the criterion is a "straw man" of sorts, because when the problem, with all its presuppositions and background assumptions is properly understood, it seems quite obvious that it is impossible to settle the dispute *given* the standard of irrefutable provability. Is this a *problem*? Once one understands that settling the dispute in this context requires satisfying a standard that is impossible to meet, there is no longer any rational doubt about how to answer the question. It cannot be settled. There is no rational doubt involved in asking whether one can do the impossible, and, hence, the question no longer poses a problem for those who understand this.[40]

In this particular case, suppose that persons X and Y are in a dispute about the truth of impression Z. In order to settle the dispute, the truth of impression Z must be picked out by a criterion of truth, which is validated by a deductive proof, which is confirmed by an *already demonstrably validated criterion* (what Sextus calls a "true" criterion). The phrase "already demonstrably validated criterion" refers to either the first criterion mentioned, in which case we have a vicious circle, or to a different criterion, in which case we are led on an infinite regress. According to the Stoic standard of irrefutable provability, neither a sound proof nor a true criterion can exist without the previous existence of the other. *This is, in effect, to say that neither exists, because it is impossible that each exists before the other.*[41] Therefore, the Stoic standard of irrefutable provability turns out to be an impossible condition. And if irrefutable provability is an impossible condition, which is presupposed as a necessary condition for settling the dispute, then it is certainly no surprise that settling the dispute is impossible. But once this is understood, there is no longer any rational doubt involved in posing the question. There is no longer any problem. The problem has been *dissolved.*

There is no more of a problem in asking, "How do you settle a dispute between individuals who claim certain impressions true or false and those who disagree?" than there is in asking, "How do you square a circle?" The former only looks like a problem when we are unclear about what is meant by "settle a dispute." The ancient problem of the criterion has a dissolution. It is a question that when properly understood, involves no rational doubt or uncertainty about its correct answer. The parallel with the question about squaring a circle is striking:

Q. How do you square a circle?
A. It is impossible to square a circle (the condition that is required to satisfy squaring a circle is impossible to meet).
Q. How do you settle a dispute between individuals who claim certain impressions true or false and those who disagree?
A. The dispute is impossible to settle (the condition necessary to satisfy settlement is impossible to meet).

When we understand what is meant by the question, which poses the ancient problem, we discover there is no *problem* at all.

One might retort with the following query. Suppose you will win a million dollars if you square a circle, and suppose that you really need a million dollars and there is no other way for you to obtain it. Wouldn't the question "How do you square a circle?" be a problem for you? Or similarly, suppose that you *want* to settle a dispute and the only way to do so is to irrefutably prove one disputant's claim to be true and the other's false. Wouldn't the question "How do you settle a dispute between individuals who claim certain impressions true or false and those who disagree?" be a problem for you? My answer is, quite simply, that it would be a problem for you in some *practical sense,* but it is not a philosophical problem because there is no rational doubt about the correct answer to the question. In both cases, the answer is clearly that you cannot!

The question that naturally arises is: what else *could* be a "settling of the dispute"? If Max Black is correct, then this question can only be answered generally because settling the dispute would seem to mean providing a rationally satisfactory justification to the disputants on the basis of their mutually accepted standard. If this is correct, then the standard will vary with the kind of disputes and disputants. What could settle the dispute would depend upon the rationally agreed upon standard for settling that dispute. Where no standard is mutually rationally acceptable, no settling is possible on the basis of such a standard. Where the standard is impossible to meet but mutually agreed upon, no settlement is possible.

There are, of course, other ways that one might settle a dispute—by force, blackmail, bribery, brainwashing, sophistical argumentation, and such. But we are concerned only with settling a dispute by *epistemically rational* means, an epistemically rational justification.

Therefore, the ancient problem of the criterion, as characterized by Sextus Empiricus dissolves when clearly understood.[42] The question about what else could settle a dispute seems, at least in part, to depend upon the kind of standard of justification that is rationally acceptable to the disputants. I will return to this question of standards in Chapter 6, but we have yet to consider the modern problem of the criterion posed by Roderick Chisholm and Nicholas Rescher.

The Modern Problem

What made the ancient problem a pseudoproblem was its impossible presupposition that only irrefutable provability could settle a dispute. We noted in Chapter 4 that what distinguishes the modern problem from its ancient counterpart is the context within which the question is posed—the presuppositions involved in each. Neither Chisholm nor Rescher presuppose Stoic epistemology in their treatment of the problem. Chisholm poses the problem in terms of his two pairs of questions:

(A) What do we know? What is the extent of our knowledge?
B) How do we decide whether we know? What are the criteria of knowledge?

Q. If you cannot answer (A) until you know the answer to (B), and you cannot answer (B) until you know the answer to (A), how can you answer either question?

We learned in the Chapter 4 that Chisholm believes that he can make an adjudication between the true and the false without employing or knowing any criterion beforehand. That is the message of particularism. Rescher believes that he can provide a plausibility argument, á la methodological pragmatism, that gives his position "solid rational warrant." Both answers concern their epistemological theories, but not the justification of such epistemological theories—at least not the kind of justification that seems necessary to settle the dispute between particularist, methodist, and skeptic.

Simply *answering* (A) and/or (B) does not deal with the problem. After all, one can "answer" a question by simply offering a semantically appropriate response. For example, one can "answer" the question, "Does God exist?" simply by responding "Yes" or "No." The term "answer" in Chisholm's characterization of the problem must have a special meaning. It must mean more than giving a correct response too, because one could give a correct answer just by luck or guesswork. "Answer" must mean either giving "an epistemically rationally justified answer" to (A) or (B) or an answer to (A) or (B) "that one can epistemically rationally justify." The difference here is between giving an answer for which one *is justified*, as opposed to *being able to justify* one's answer to (A) or (B). Both involve metalevel justification but only the latter interpretation, I believe, is correct. Here's why.

If we interpret "answer" to mean giving a response for which one *is justified*, then both Chisholm and Rescher may be able to satisfy this condition, yet it would not settle the dispute. Indeed, both Chisholm and Rescher believe that they *are justified* in their epistemological positions, but neither *can justify* his answer to the skeptic. "Answer" must mean "to be able to rationally justify."

Now suppose that I do know such a thing as that this is a hand. What more is necessary to "answer" either (A) or (B)? Well, I suppose that it means being able to rationally justify my claim to know that this is a hand. What is involved in such a rational justification? The skeptic seems to be claiming that the *only* acceptable kind of rational justification for such a claim is, or at least relies on, an "answer" to (B). And of course, "answer" here means "rationally justified answer," and "rationally justified answer," in this case, implies an answer to (A).

This characterization of "answer" and "rationally justify" begins to sound like another impossible condition. Each "answer" [to (A) or (B)] requires the prior answering of the other, and since both *cannot* be prior to each other, neither is answerable. If our condition for an "answer" to either question is impossible, in principle, to meet, then of course an answer is indeed impossible. The claim of the skeptic is not that knowledge is impossible, but rather that it is impossible to *justify* a knowledge claim.[43]

Since the conditions necessary for answering the question are in principle impossible to meet, then again there is no rational doubt about how to answer the question, and, hence, no problem here either. The modern problem *dissolves* much like its ancient counterpart. Neither Chisholm nor Rescher seems to appreciate the fact that there is no real problem to a question that involves no rational doubt. The reason for this, I believe, is that the conditions set for an acceptable "answer" to the question are not as *obviously impossible* to an inquirer as are the conditions for squaring a circle. It takes some investigation and analysis before one discovers this impossible condition, and further thought about the nature of a philosophical problem before one realizes that one must have rational doubt about a question for it to be a problem. Hence, we cannot fault them for finding the question problematic.

For example, if someone were perplexed about how to "solve" the "problem" of how one squares a circle, it would be sufficient to demonstrate to that individual that the question asks us to do what is, in principle, impossible to do; and thus there is nothing puzzling about our inability to square a circle. The problem dissolves once one sees that the question involves no rational doubt. And so too with the modern problem of the criterion; when the question is fully understood, the apparent problem dissolves.[44]

Recently, Sharon Ryan suggested that my dissolution of the problem looks like an endorsement of the skeptic's position.[45] After all, it is the *skeptic* who claims that you cannot answer (A) and you cannot answer (B), and I seem to be supporting this thesis by my recognition that it is impossible to "answer" (A) or (B). She asks, "So why not think the problem has been *solved* by the skeptic rather than *dissolved* by Amico?" Her question deserves attention.

I have described the problem of the criterion as a metaepistemological problem about how one can *justify* a knowledge claim. We should keep in mind that justifying a knowledge claim is different from knowing that we know. We could have second order knowledge (knowledge of our knowledge) without being able to justify our claim to this knowledge. Just as, on a first order level, we could know that A is F without being *able* to justify our claim that A is F. Just as knowing does not imply knowing that we know,[46] so too knowing does not imply that we *can justify* what we know. For example, I might know that in a right-angled triangle, the sum of the square of the two sides is equal to the square of the hypotenuse, without being able to justify my claim. I may have forgotten how to demonstrate or justify what I know, but I may know it nonetheless. I may posses the evidence without being able to produce it or demonstrate how it supports my claim.

Anyhow, the problem of the criterion concerns how we settle the dispute about knowledge claims made by the particularist, methodist, and skeptic. Each holds an epistemological position, which each may *be* justified in believing. But *solving* the problem of the criterion requires settling the dispute and settling the dispute seems to require (according to the skeptic anyhow) *justifying* one's position. And again, according to the skeptic, the only kind of justification that is acceptable requires meeting an impossible condition. The skeptic's *position* involves at least three claims: (1) in order to answer (A) you need to know already the answer to (B); (2) in order to answer (B) you need to know already the answer to (A); (3) you cannot answer either (A) or (B). This position, like particularism and methodism, requires justification in order for us to settle the dispute. Each disputant can claim to *be* justified in her epistemological position, but that will not settle the dispute. The skeptic can no more justify her position (i.e., meet her own impossible condition) than can the particularist or methodist. Hence, the skeptic's position could never be a solution to the problem of the criterion.

What I point out in the dissolution of the problem is that the conditions set for settling the dispute are, in principle, impossible to meet. By doing this, I do not claim that the skeptic is wrong here. I do not claim that there is no problem because the skeptic is wrong about the condition set for settling the dispute. Meeting the condition, albeit impossible, may be sufficient to settle the dispute. I point out that *if* meeting this condition is *required* for settling the dispute, as the skeptic seems to suppose, then it is no surprise that settling the dispute is impossible. Indeed, the problem, in this context, then *dissolves*, because there is no longer any rational doubt about how to answer the question. You cannot settle the dispute.

Our skeptic, however, may also be a metaepistemological skeptic—one who claims that we cannot justify any claims to knowledge, be they claims to know or claims to its impossibility. Such a skeptic would subscribe to the view that the impossible condition for justifying knowledge claims is a necessary condition for such justification. This is a meta-metalevel claim concerning what metaepistemic conditions are necessary to justify a knowledge claim.

Does my claim—the skeptic's condition for justifying a knowledge claim is impossible to meet—make me a metaepistemological skeptic? No, not necessarily, because in doing so, I am not claiming to accept this condition as a necessary condition for justification.[47] I am merely pointing out that it is an impossible condition and that therefore the problem posed by the skeptic and apparently accepted by particularist and methodist alike, is really not a problem. But our investigation into the issue surrounding the dissolved problem of the criterion, that is, of settling the dispute between our disputants, does not end here because this impossible condition *may* only be a sufficient condition for settling the dispute. There may be other conditions that are also sufficient, yet are not impossible to meet.

So our questions do not end here. On the contrary, I think the really interesting questions begin here. If this impossible condition is merely sufficient for an "answer" to either question, then we may be able to make some progress towards settling the dispute. This avenue will lead us to many more concerning the presuppositions of the skeptic, and eventually to a repudiation of the problem of the criterion and a critique of skepticism.

NOTES

1. Ernest Sosa, "The Raft and the Pyramid," in *Midwest Studies in Philosophy*, vol. 5, eds. P. French, T. Uehling, and H. Wettstein (Minneapolis: University of Minnesota Press, 1980), 3–26.
2. Ibid., 3.
3. Sosa, "Foundations of Foundationalism," 552.
4. Ibid. 558.
5. In so far as particularism is concerned with first order knowledge claims, we can consider it as an epistemological thesis, although its role in the problem of the criterion will be all metaepistemological.
6. Roderick Firth, "Coherence, Certainty, and Epistemic Priority," *Journal of Philosophy* 61 (1964): 549.
7. By "prior," I do not necessarily mean temporally prior; knowledge of P might be logically prior to knowledge of Q in the following sense: knowledge of P might be a logically necessary condition for knowledge of Q. If knowledge of P is a logically necessary condition for knowledge of Q, then necessarily if Q is known then P is known, but not vice versa. The thesis of epistemic dependence covers both possible positions.
8. This argument was inspired by a discussion I had with Lou Goble during a paper presentation at the 1990 Northwest Philosophy Conference.
9. Paul Moser, *Knowledge and Evidence* (Cambridge: Cambridge University Press, 1989), 264.
10. Nelson Goodman, *Fact, Fiction and Forecast* (Cambridge: Harvard University Press, 1955), 67.
11. Moser, *Knowledge*, 264.
12. Susan Haack, "Theories of Knowledge: An Analytic Framework," *Proceedings of the Aristotelian Society* 83 (1982–83): 151.
13. Michael DePaul, "Reflective Equilibrium and Foundationalism," *American Philosophical Quarterly* 23, no. 1 (1986): 59.
14. Whether Moser does achieve this as well or better than Rescher or Chisholm is a matter for another day. It would require an analysis of his epistemology, which is beyond the scope of this inquiry.
15. See Robert Lehe, "Coherence and the Problem of the Criterion," *Idealistic Studies* 19, no. 2 (1989): 112–20.
16. F. H. Bradley, *Appearance and Reality* (Oxford: Oxford University Press, 1893), 120, my emphasis.
17. This is Robert Lehe's point in "Coherence."
18. See R. Amico, "On the Vindication of Deduction and Induction," *Austral-*

asian Journal of Philosophy 64, no. 3 (1986): 322–30, for a more complete exposition of vicious circularity.

19. W. C. Salmon, *The Foundations of Scientific Inference* (Pittsburgh, Penn.: University of Pittsburgh Press, 1966), 15. For a more explicit and detailed account of rule circularity, see Amico, "Vindication."

20. C. D. Broad, "Mr. Bradley on Truth and Reality," *Mind* 23 (1914): 349–70; Rescher, *Coherence Theory*, 45; Bertrand Russell, *The Problems of Philosophy* (Oxford: Oxford University Press, 1912), 122–23.

21. Russell, 123.

22. Ibid.

23. Lehe, 119.

24. Stich makes a similar point concerning what it is for something to be a belief. He claims that "it is part of what it is to be a belief with a given intentional characterization, part of the concept of such a belief, if you will, to interact with other beliefs in a rational way—a way which more or less *mirrors the laws of logic*." [See Stephen Stich, *The Fragmentation of Reason* (Cambridge,: MIT Press, 1990), 37.]

25. Haack, "Theories of Knowledge." This is Susan Haack's appellative for a theory that combines foundationalism and coherentism.

26. Aristotle, *Posterior Analytics*, Bk. I, chap. 3, in *The Basic Works of Aristotle*, 113–14; my emphasis.

27. Chisholm, *TK*, 2d ed., 19.

28. See K. Lehrer, *Knowledge* (Oxford: Oxford University Press, 1974), 15–16; F. L. Will, *Induction and Justification* (Ithaca, N.Y.: Cornell University Press, 1974), 176–85; R. Foley, "Inferential Justification and the Infinite Regress," *American Philosophical Quarterly* 15 (1978): 311–16; J. F. Post, "Infinite Regresses of Justification and of Explanation," *Philosophical Studies* 38 (1980): 31–52; L. Bonjour, "The Coherence Theory of Empirical Knowledge," *Philosophical Studies* 30 (1976): 282; C. Ginet, *Knowledge, Memory and Perception* (Dordrecht, Holland: Reidel, 1975), 53; J. Pollock, *Knowledge and Justification* (Princeton, N.J.: Princeton University Press, 1974), 25–29.

29. See Sosa, "The Raft and the Pyramid"; B. Aune, "Remarks on Argument by Chisholm," *Philosophical Studies* 23 (1972): 327–34; J. Harker, "Can There Be an Infinite Regress of Justified Beliefs?" *Australasian Journal of Philosophy* 62, no. 3 (1984): 255–64.

30. Harker.

31. Recall that in Chapter 3 we noted that Moser has refined this objection to accommodate fallibilist theories of justification by linking justification to evidence rather than truth. This refinement, however, will not change the import of Harker's point.

32. Harker, 263.

33. Aune, 327–34.

34. Sosa, "Foundations of Foundationalism," 547.

35. This point is also made by Harker, but not in connection with the problem of the criterion, and by W. Alston in "Epistemic Circularity," reprinted in Alston, *Epistemic Justification* (Ithaca, N.Y.: Cornell University Press, 1989), 345.

36. Since all dissolutions involve realizing the impossibility of a solution and hence denying one's earlier presupposition that there is a solution, and since all repudiations involve denying a presupposition of the question that posed the problem, all dissolutions are, in this sense, also repudiations. But the reverse is not true; not all repudiations are dissolutions. For example, in *Euthyphro*, Euthyphro could have repudiated the problem posed by Socrates in the question "What is Piety?" by denying Socrates' presupposition that Piety has a single essential nature. But such a repudiation would not be a dissolution to the problem. I am indebted to Richard Feldman for this insight.

37. Rescher, *Methodological Pragmatism*, 18.

38. Sextus Empiricus, *PH* 1.257.

39. Max Black, *Language and Philosophy* (Ithaca, N.Y.: Cornell University Press, 1949), 63.

40. Is, then, the problem of the criterion decisive against claims to irrefutable provability? To say that it is, is only to say that it is decisive against claims to the impossible, and, hence, I believe the question is otiose.

41. One might ask if it is possible to interpret Stoic standard of irrefutable provability in terms *other* than that of *temporal priority*. Setting aside the question of whether there is any textual support for this suggestion, I think we can respond as follows. As I suggested earlier in this chapter (note 6), one could argue that one (proof or criterion) is *logically* prior to the other in the sense that one is a logically necessary condition of the other. But this would not help the skeptic, because logical priority is an asymmetrical relationship like temporal priority. If knowledge of P is a logically necessary condition for knowledge of Q, then necessarily if Q is known, then P is known, *but not vice versa*. Hence the standard, interpreted in either way, is in principle impossible to meet.

42. To the extent that Montaigne's problem is the same as Sextus's, the dissolution would run the same way.

43. My remarks concerning temporal priority and logical priority in note 41 of this chapter hold true for the modern problem as well.

44. One might argue that these conditions come from what it takes to show cogently that one has knowledge; so the inadequacy is perhaps not with the problem, but with our notion of showing that we have knowledge. The problem of the criterion would then be important for what it illustrates about our ordinary notion of showing that we have knowledge. The defect would then be in the latter notion, not in the problem of the criterion. (My thanks to Paul Moser for this response.) This objection is actually on the right track, because even if both the ancient and the modern version of the problem of the criterion can be dissolved, as I suggest, we are still left with the difficulty of how we justify knowledge claims. But for reasons that will become clear in Chapter 6, I address this metaepistemological question, after having first established that there is a dissolution, to both the ancient and modern problems.

45. Sharon Ryan's comments came to me as her response to my paper on this topic delivered at the Tri-State Philosophical Association meeting, Spring 1990, in Erie, Penn. Her essay is forthcoming in *On Knowing and the Known*, ed. Ken Lucey (New York: Prometheus Books, 1993).

46. See Chisholm, *TK*, 3d ed., 99–100. I agree with him on this point.

47. Indeed, in the next chapter the differences between myself and the skeptic will become apparent. For now, let me say, as a partial response to Ryan, that we disagree about what conditions are necessary and/or sufficient for justifying a knowledge claim.

Chapter 6

Skepticism and the Problem of the Criterion

By asking ourselves whether the modern skeptic's impossible condition for justifying a knowledge claim is sufficient, merely sufficient, necessary, or both necessary and sufficient for settling the dispute between our three disputants, we begin to question the status and reasonability of one of the skeptic's presuppositions. The attempts by both Rescher and Moser to deal with the problem of the criterion are instructive in this regard. Both attempts endorse a metaepistemological coherence theory of justification (of one sort or another), which calls into question the principle of epistemic priority at the metalevel. Rescher's thesis is insightful in that he recognizes that the problem of the criterion is, in principle, impossible to solve, and so he tries to offer an answer that *comes close* to, but falls short of satisfying the skeptic's condition for an acceptable justification. Moser, on the other hand, questions the skeptic's presupposition of the principle of epistemic dependence by claiming that justification does not proceed linearly but rather latitudinally by bringing principles and particulars together in reflective equilibrium. Both theses are insightful, in my view, because they look to *alternatives* not circumscribed by how the skeptic poses the problem. I think their defect is that they do not take this process far enough to be really effective.

Most philosophers who have tried to deal with the problem of the criterion—at least those with whom I am familiar—seem to accept the problem *as the skeptic poses it*. I believe that this is a mistake. The positions of both particularist and methodist are scrutinized meticulously and each is asked for impossible justification. Both Chisholm and Rescher present admirable theories in response and attempt thereby to relieve their epistemological angst. But in making this prodigious effort, a more critical examination of the skeptic's position has been overlooked. The strategy I plan to adopt requires taking the skeptic *very seriously* (rather than ruling out skepticism, as Chisholm does, at the outset of inquiry) and examining what presuppositions the skeptic makes in maintaining her position. After all, if the skeptic is going to claim that the kind of justification of knowledge claims offered by Chisholm and

Rescher are unacceptable, then we have a right to ask why. We have a right to ask why the skeptic thinks her impossible condition is acceptable and why he/she thinks that only such a condition is acceptable. We must find the skeptic's reasons acceptable in order to accept such constraints on our attempts to justify knowledge claims.

Why should we accept the skeptic's conditions on an acceptable answer to Chisholm's pair of questions (A) and (B) (see page 76)? The skeptic claims that in order to justify one's claim to know the answer to (A), (e.g., that I have a left hand), I must know the answer to (B); that is, I must know some criterion or method by means of which I can identify this as a case of actual knowledge as opposed to merely apparent knowledge. Why? If I knew such a criterion and *if I could apply it correctly*, then I could be absolutely guaranteed that this particular was an instance of knowledge because I could directly (deductively) check my knowledge claim against a known criterion. The skeptic would argue similarly in the case of a knowledge claim to (B). In order to justify one's claim to know the answer to (B) (e.g., to know anything that I clearly and distinctly perceive), I must know the answer to (A); that is, I must know some actual instances of knowledge so that I can test the criterion by its fidelity to this knowledge and so ensure absolutely, *if I can apply the instances to the criterion correctly*, that the criterion is the true criterion of knowledge.

But knowing the answer to (A) or (B) is no absolute guarantee that one will apply it flawlessly to answer the other question.[1] One could make a mistake. Hence, it would be an error to think that simply meeting the skeptic's condition would be *sufficient* to settle the dispute. Even if the skeptic were correct that in order to answer (A) one needs to already know the answer to (B) and vice versa, simply meeting this condition would not provide us with a "logically airtight guarantee"[2] of its correctness. Meeting this impossible condition, then, by itself, is not sufficient to settle the dispute. The skeptic could claim that knowing an answer to (A) or (B) is a necessary condition for answering the other, because only then is it *possible* to answer the other correctly. This would mean that meeting an impossible condition is a necessary condition for the possibility of answering either (A) or (B) correctly and settling the dispute. Even though the condition is impossible to meet, it could be such a necessary condition and this would spell trouble for the particularist and methodist. But if it is a necessary condition, the skeptic owes us some *reason* for or *justification* of this claim. It seems that such a claim rests on some kind of metaepistemological presupposition about the nature and attainability of knowledge or justified belief. I agree with Fumerton's claim that "the arguments of the skeptic most often *presuppose* metaepistemological positions but there is often far too little explicit discussion of the nature of knowledge or justified belief."[3] This leads us back, then, to our plan to examine the skeptic's presuppositions.

Another reason for adopting this strategy concerns the very nature of disputes or disagreements. In many cases of disagreement, if not all, and certainly in this case, the disputants must share some common assumptions if only about some of the concepts invoked in the disagreement. It seems difficult to see how two individuals could have a disagreement without sharing *some* common assumptions or presuppositions, because without some such common ground, even communication would be frustrated. I believe that we can come to understand disagreements better by uncovering and understanding where disputants agree. What is the common ground? It will be my contention that the skeptic cannot avoid making certain presuppositions that undermine her skeptical thesis and that meeting her impossible condition is neither sufficient nor necessary for settling the dispute. If this turns out to be correct, then the skeptic's position will be less reasonable that that of her competitors. But now I am getting a bit ahead of myself. We must first be clear about what the skeptic's presuppositions are, and to do that we must first explain what a presupposition is.

PRESUPPOSITIONS

According to Soames, there are three basic approaches to the nature of presupposition: Frege's approach with logical presupposition, Strawson's approach with expressive presupposition, and Stalnaker's approach with pragmatic presupposition.[4] A closely related notion is that of contextual implication.[5] While Strawson's account is probably most well known—S presupposes S' = def. the truth of S' is a necessary condition of the truth or falsity of the statement that S[6]—it faces some rather serious criticism[7] as does the Fregean account.[8]

In Chapter 1, I drew upon Stalnaker's work on pragmatic presupposition to characterize a philosophical problem. As I explained there, Stalnaker characterizes presupposition as a propositional attitude or disposition of a person, usually exemplified by linguistic behavior. *People*, not sentences, make presuppositions.

> To presuppose a proposition in the pragmatic sense is to take its truth for granted, and to assume that others involved in the context do the same. . . . The set of all the presuppositions made by a person in a given context determines a class of possible worlds, the ones consistent with all the presuppositions. This class sets the boundaries of the linguistic situation.[9]

There is a striking similarity between Stalnaker's notion of pragmatic presupposition and Hungerland's notion of contextual implication. On Hungerland's account, if S presupposes S' in the Strawsonian sense, then the speaker, in making the statement that S, contextually implies that she believes that S'. For example, in stating "All my children are asleep," I normally contextually imply that I believe that I have children.[10] In both cases, *people* make presuppositions and contextual implications. It is not a relationship between statements or propositions, but rather concerns the *beliefs* of the speaker. Rather than explore the differences, subtle or otherwise, between pragmatic presupposition and contextual implication, I shall simply stay with Stalnaker's notion in this analysis.

To this array of approaches to the nature of presupposition, I would like to add one more that will help to explicate the idea of how one belief can be based upon another. Consider the following stipulative definition of *epistemic* presupposition:

> EPP: P' is an epistemic presupposition of P for S = def. at least part of S's justification for believing in P relies on believing in or accepting P' (i.e., relies on employing P' in the justification of P).

An example will help to illustrate the difference between pragmatic presupposition and epistemic presupposition. Suppose that I make the statement "The house on the hill is haunted." And suppose that in making this statement, I *pragmatically* presuppose that there is a house on the hill, because I am, in so stating, taking its truth for granted (believe it is true). Suppose, further, that I believe that the house on the hill is haunted (call this proposition P) because I saw ghosts there last week (call this proposition P'). P' is an *epistemic* presupposition of P for me because at least part of my justification for believing that P is that I believe that P'. Whether my justification is adequate or not is not important to this notion of presupposition. It is enough that I *take* there to be a connection between P and P' such that I believe that accepting P' at least partially justifies me in accepting P.

P' can be both an epistemic presupposition of P for me and a pragmatic presupposition for me. While pragmatic presupposition picks out those propositions whose *truth* one takes for granted, epistemic presupposition picks out those propositions that are perceived to be *epistemically* related. We can now employ these two notions of presupposition to the position of the skeptic.

AGAINST SKEPTICISM

By *ultimate canon of deductive logic*, I mean that canon selected to validate all other canons or principles of logic. In any selected system, there will always be at least one canon that itself cannot be validated, but that can be used to validate all the others. Different canons can be employed in different selected systems, and they can be complex. In the case of the skeptic, let P' = the skeptic's ultimate canon(s) of deductive logic. Let P = the claim that if her impossible condition were met, then it would be possible to answer (A) or (B) because, if one could apply it correctly, its truth would be deductively guaranteed.

For example, suppose our known criterion is all Xs are Ys. We correctly apply our particular instance—Z is an X—to the criterion and conclude that Z is a Y. Abstracting criteria of knowledge from particular cases would seem to be a more difficult matter and more prone to error than applying particulars to criteria. The problem of applying one's knowledge is a difficult one for the skeptic here. But it seems to me that if we ask ourselves *why* the skeptic requires prior knowledge of both criteria and particulars to answer either question even though one could err in applying each once in possession of such knowledge, the answer must be that the condition has intuitive appeal to the skeptic as a necessary condition for the possibility of answering (A) or (B).

Why is this so? Well, one possibility is that she might argue that if we can rule out error in application, then we could have a *deductive proof*. This reasoning would fit in nicely with that of Sextus Empiricus who speaks of preferring one impression to another "either uncritically and without proof or critically and with proof."[11] In claiming that you cannot answer (A) until you answer (B) and you cannot answer (B) until you answer (A), the skeptic has not committed herself to the claim that having an answer to either one is sufficient to answer the other, only that it is necessary. Another response that comes to mind is that the skeptic simply finds her condition to be intuitively correct, period. Let me begin by assuming the former answer—reliance on logic—and later I will deal with the latter possibility about intuition.

FIRST POSSIBILITY—RELIANCE ON LOGIC

We can see that P' is an epistemic presupposition of P for the skeptic as well as a pragmatic presupposition. This is because in the case of the former, at least part of her justification for believing in P relies on accepting P' (i.e., relies on employing P' in the justification of P) and because, in the case of the latter, in stating P, she takes the truth of P' for granted and assumes that others involved in the context do the same. Recall that P' = the skeptic's ultimate canon(s) of deductive logic; and P = the claim that if her impossible condition were met, then it would be possible to answer (A) or (B). (If one could apply it correctly, its truth would be deductively guaranteed.) Hence, P' is one of the skeptic's epistemic and pragmatic presuppositions.

This finding becomes important when we realize that the very standard that is both pragmatically and epistemically presupposed by the skeptic in claiming that answering (A) or (B) is impossible, cannot itself be justified by satisfying the skeptic's standard. In other words, the skeptic cannot meet her very own condition—the condition that she introduces to argue that neither particularism nor methodism can answer (A) or (B). How does the skeptic justify her reliance on and acceptance of the canons of deductive logic? If we accept such canons as well, then it will be incumbent upon us to examine our justification for accepting them. But here I think we have an advantage over the skeptic.

Let us suppose that we claim to know or be justified in believing that "if P then Q, and P, therefore Q" is a valid deductive rule. If this is one of our basic, primitive, or ultimate, rules, then it has been shown that one cannot justify it by means of an argument (either deductively or pragmatically),[12] that is, it cannot be shown to be valid in a nonquestion-begging way. Does this mean that we cannot justify our claim that we know Modus Ponens (MP) is a valid rule? I think not. Some think that our *intuition* of the validity of MP justifies our claim that we know MP is a valid rule. Some might also claim that MP needs no justification.

When is a call for justification rationally appropriate? Max Black claimed that "a demand for justification is normally taken to imply a *discrepancy with some standard*. And a satisfactory justification is one which neutralizes the apparent discrepancy by showing it to be consistent with, or deducible from, the relevant standard."[13] This claim is so broad that it allows for a call for justification whenever anyone with *any* standard claims discrepancy with their standard. However, even this characterization seems too restrictive because one could call for a justification of some claim even if one has no "acceptable standard." One may simply be asking for another person's reasons for claiming something without having any standard oneself. Hence, Black's characterization seems too restrictive. Almost any conditions may be rationally appropriate to call for a justification of some claim. And so, if, by the claim that MP needs no justification, it is meant that a call for justification in this case is not rationally appropriate, then some reason would need to be given in support of this claim. If this is not what is meant, then I am not sure just what such a claim means.

With MP, it is not that a justification through argument is not needed, but that it cannot be obtained. But our inability to provide such a justification has not led most philosophers to be skeptical about MP (including our skeptic).

Why not? Perhaps it is because our intuition about MP is so strong that it seems to provide us with a *kind* of justification for our claims about MP that is different from the kind of justification obtained through a validating argument. There seems to be a point of similarity here between our inability to provide a justification by argument for our knowledge claim in answer to either (A) or (B) and in the case of our ultimate canons of logic (MP in this case). Perhaps there is also a parallel between what it is about MP that justifies us in our claims about it and what it is about an answer to either (A) or (B) that justifies us in our claims about it.

One might argue that what it is about MP that justifies us in our claims that it is a valid rule are our logical intuitions. For example, Pollock argues that our logical intuitions provide prima facie justification for our acceptance of a priori judgments, just as our faculty of sight gives us prima facie justification for our acceptance of certain perceptual judgments. Some of our logical intuitions may be overridden by using other logical intuitions against them.[14] Where argument fails to give a justification, our logical intuitions justify our claim that MP is a valid rule and, for example, Modus Morons (MM)[15] is not a valid rule.

Is there anything about our answer to either (A) or (B) which parallels the claim about MP? One might argue that there is a parallel. One could claim that we have certain epistemic intuitions that justify our answer to (A) or (B). For example, I might claim to have an answer to (B) by claiming to know anything that I clearly and distinctly perceive. What would justify my claim? My intuitions. I might even claim that to think contrary to these intuitions would be just as irrational as it would be to think otherwise in logic and accept, for example, MM. I am not endorsing this position here, but simply pointing out that there is an alternative way of justifying an answer to (A) or (B).

This suggestion would be a kind of justification that is different from giving an argument; one could appeal to intuition to justify an answer to (A) or (B). If someone like the skeptic were to claim that she does not have such intuitions about the answer to (A) or (B), there seems to be no way of rationally convincing her otherwise. The same is true in logic. As Lewis Carroll and Rudolf Carnap have pointed out, one could never rationally convince someone who was deductively blind of the validity of MP.[16] Thus, one might argue that the epistemic status of one's answer to (A) or (B) is in no more trouble than MP.

The skeptic accepts MP and uses deductive logic to argue against both the methodist and the particularist. The skeptic cannot justify her reliance and acceptance of these canons by means of the very standard she sets up to criticize others. The standard is, in principle, impossible to meet. Chisholm believed that his position was no worse (no less arbitrary) than any of the others; that the skeptic's position has no more to recommend it than the others do. But I think that Chisholm is wrong here. It seems to me that we do have good reason to believe that meeting some impossible condition is not the only way to justify our knowledge claims.

The important question at hand, then, seems to be "What means of justification of some knowledge claim are or count as good/acceptable/rational justifications of such claims?" Here the skeptic is claiming that only a justification that is in principle impossible to give is acceptable. Indeed, if this were the only way to justify such a claim, then the skeptic would not be able to justify her claim that answering (A) or (B) is impossible because such a claim relies on certain canons of deductive logic that the skeptic cannot so justify.

First Objection

Now the skeptic may have an answer to our criticism. I have argued that the skeptic must accept that there are other acceptable methods for justifying a knowledge claim (other than her impossible condition), such as intuition in the case of logic, because she employs and accepts logical canons to argue her position against opponents. If the skeptic's criticism rests on propositions that she cannot justify, then her argument has no force against her opponents. It is an arbitrary and unsupported claim. To the extent that her claim has force, she must admit that she is justified in believing it even though she cannot justify it by means of argument. The skeptic may reply that she cannot justify her assumptions and that she too is caught on the wheel of her own making. The skeptic is not immune to these epistemological dilemmas either.

I think that this response is misleading and incorrect. The point that I have been trying to make is that the problem of the criterion is only a problem if one accepts all those propositions that are pragmatically and epistemically presupposed by the skeptic as she poses the problem. I have tried to show that the problem that the skeptic characterizes, when clearly understood, has a dissolution. Furthermore, this dissolution leads us to question what meta-epistemological assumptions underlie the skeptic's position. By trying to enter into a dialogue with the skeptic, we are then entitled to ask for a justification for her claim that only meeting an impossible condition can justify a knowledge claim to (A) or (B).

The skeptic needs to justify her claim before she can convince anyone that there is rational doubt about which propositions to accept and reject. Without this rational doubt, there is no problem about whether to accept or reject particularists' and methodists' claims to knowledge.

The skeptic, then, is not caught on a wheel of her own making until there is a problem. So, if she claims that she is not justified in her assumptions, then we need not have any reason to accept her claim that (A) or (B) is not answerable, and hence, there is no problem about whether to accept or reject her disputant's knowledge claims. If she claims that she is justified in her assumptions, then she must tell us how. If she claims that she *is* justified but cannot justify her position (certainly not in terms of her own condition for acceptable justifications), then two points can be made.

First, if the skeptic cannot justify by means of her own impossible condition her claim that only meeting some impossible condition constitutes an acceptable justification of some knowledge claim, then her claim that such a condition is the only acceptable condition is undermined. This puts the skeptic at an epistemological disadvantage when compared to the particularist and methodist. For while both the particularist and methodist also cannot justify their respective knowledge claims in terms of the skeptic's impossible condition, the need to meet such a condition is called into question by the skeptic's inability to meet her own condition.

Second, consider the following principle of justification:

JP: If S *is* justified in believing that P at least partially on the basis of Q, and S believes that S is justified in believing that P at least partially on the basis of Q, and Q is an epistemic presupposition of P for S, then S accepts Q as a means of at least partially justifying S's belief that P.

If the skeptic believes that her ultimate canons of deductive logic are at least partially a means of justifying her belief that only meeting some impossible condition can justify an answer to (A) or (B), then not only does she believe that there are other sufficient conditions for justifying a knowledge claim, but she is employing a means of justification other than one that meets her impossible condition. In other words, by relying on the canons of deductive logic to justify her claim about acceptable justifications, she ipso facto contradicts her claim about acceptable justifications.

In what sense is the skeptic's claim self-undermining? The claim is not strictly self-refuting, nor is it pragmatically self-refuting in Burnyeat's sense.[17] But consider the following stipulative definition of epistemic self-refutation, which, I believe, captures the skeptic's inconsistency:

ES-R: S's claim that P is epistemically self-refuting = def. P' is an epistemic presupposition of P for S at t and believing that P' is inconsistent with believing that P.

For example, if the skeptic claims that only meeting her impossible condition can justify one's knowledge claim (call this P), and she relies on intuition or deductive logic (call this P′) to justify her claim that P (i.e., P′ is an epistemic presupposition of P for the skeptic), then her belief that P′ justifies the claim that P is inconsistent with her belief that P. Hence, her claim that P is epistemically self-refuting.

It is like the occultist with the crystal ball who claims that only his crystal ball can tell us the truth. When asked what justifies this claim, he says that he read his tea leaves and they told him so. The fact that the occultist relies on tea leaves to justify a claim about the crystal ball and believes it to be another source of truth is inconsistent with his claim that the crystal ball is the only source of truth.

So, the fact that the skeptic's claim is epistemically self-refuting not only undermines her position, but it also strengthens the position of the particularist and methodist alike. For if there are other sufficient conditions for justifying a knowledge claim, then their position is vindicated and we have some reason for preferring methodism and particularism over skepticism.

Second Objection

One might argue that *if* one *were* to accept the ultimate canons of logic (as we all do), then the skeptic has made her point—nothing short of meeting her impossible condition is acceptable as a justification of a knowledge claim. However, if we accept the ultimate canons of logic as justified, then we ipso facto accept that there are claims that do not meet the skeptic's impossible condition that *are justified* and can be used *to justify* other claims. This, in effect, is an admission that there are other sufficient conditions for justifying a knowledge claim and it opens the door on the question of what should count as an acceptable/rational justification and what should not.

Third Objection

The skeptic might respond by saying that she *is* justified in her skeptical claim—even that she knows it to be true—for her skeptical claim does not preclude this first order justification or knowledge. The claim is that *any* such claims to first order knowledge cannot be justified unless they meet her impossible condition. The skeptic is denying the possibility of metajustification—even for herself.

Why should we accept this claim? Isn't the skeptic's claim *completely unsupported* unless she can give us *some* reason to believe it? One might argue, in the skeptic's defense, that the skeptic can make these claims *merely for the sake of argument*, and, hence, need not provide any further support or reasons. While we can agree with her that meeting her impossible condition is impossible, we need some reason to think that this is problematic—that it somehow spells trouble for us, because such a claim must create rational doubt in our minds in order to be a problem for us. So the strategy of standing her ground, digging in her heels and simply sticking to an unsupported claim—that only meeting her impossible condition will settle the dispute—will not do. As I stated earlier, for there to be a problem at all, there must be rational doubt. Unsupported claims provide me with no rational doubt.[18]

Fourth Objection

At this point, the skeptic may claim that she is justified and that the canons of deductive logic partially justify her claim that meeting her condition is necessary to settle the dispute (i.e., she epistemically and pragmatically presupposes the canons of logic in making her claim). But so what! *Logical* intuitions are intuitions we *all* accept—particularist, methodist, and skeptic. This feature makes them different from intuitions peculiar to the methodist or the particularist—intuitions about which there is great disagreement.

Logical intuitions are innocent, whereas the intuitions of the particularist and methodist are guilty. Hence, the skeptic may rely on such intuitions as first order justification for her skeptical claim and not be compelled to satisfy her own requirements for second order justification. After all, these intuitions have not been called into question; we all accept them.[19]

My reply to such an objection is that simply the fact that we all share these logical intuitions (if indeed we do) is not what justifies us in accepting them. And even if one were to argue that such agreement is constitutive of justification or one way to justify a claim, such a position would not be of help to the skeptic because she would then be admitting that there are acceptable means of justification other than meeting her impossible condition. We cannot separate logical intuitions from other kinds of intuitions simply because we all share them. They are intuitions that the skeptic has appealed to as another means of justification. If appeal to intuition is *sometimes* a means of acceptable justification for a knowledge claim, then the condition set by the skeptic is not a necessary condition for justification. And if, by the skeptic's own admission, it is not a necessary condition, then the skeptic's position that *only* meeting some impossible condition is acceptable, is untenable and *much* less reasonable than some form of methodism or particularism. Recall that earlier we established that meeting the skeptic's impossible condition was not a sufficient condition for justifying a knowledge claim. It seems now that the skeptic's impossible condition is neither sufficient nor necessary for justifying a knowledge claim.

SECOND POSSIBILITY—RELIANCE ON INTUITION

The other possibility is that the skeptic is relying solely on the intuitiveness of her claim. Logic is not presupposed in her case, but rather she bases her claim about what is required to answer each question solely on intuition. But this move will not extricate her from the difficulties discussed earlier. Either the skeptic expects the methodist and particularist simply to accept her unsupported skeptical claim or to accept intuition as an acceptable means of justifying her skeptical claim. To use the vernacular of Sextus, either the skeptic makes a claim uncritically and without justification or she makes it critically and with justification. If the skeptic makes it uncritically, then her claim does not create rational doubt about how to answer (A) or (B). For example, if I am a particularist and I present my thesis on how to answer (A) and (B), and the skeptic calls "foul" because I have not met her impossible condition, then for this to be a problem for me, I must find her *reason* for requiring her impossible condition something that raises rational doubt in me about how to answer (A) or (B). Why would *only* having a prior answer to each question be acceptable? The skeptic must support this claim. If she claims that intuition justifies her skeptical claim, then she is accepting and using intuition to justify the claim. Intuition becomes a means of justification for the skeptic and, hence, her epistemic and pragmatic presupposition about her intuition contradicts the very skeptical thesis she avers.

First Objection

The skeptic could claim that intuition can be used for first order justification but not for metajustification because metajustification is impossible. But such a strategy requires that she provide a reason why one form of justification can be used at one level but not at another. To be sure, our methodist, who claims that intuition justifies his claim to know whatever he clearly and distinctly perceives, would be particularly interested in hearing the skeptic's reason here. On the face of it, I can see no good reason to accept a method of justification for one level and reject it, in principle, for another level.

Second Objection

The skeptic could claim that intuition is only an acceptable method of justifying a claim *to oneself*, but not an acceptable method of justifying a claim to others. Intuition *makes her justified* in believing her claim, but intuition cannot be used *to justify* her claim to others. The distinction here is between *being* justified and *justifying*. This is the dilemma that all of the disputants find themselves in, and that explains why they are at an impasse. But if I become justified in my claim because of my reliance on intuition, then according to the principle of justification (JP), I accept this method as a means of justifying my belief. There is an important difference between being justified in a belief and justifying a belief by argument. It is the difference between a state and an activity.[20]

The skeptic will find no use for this distinction. Here is why. The problem of the criterion arises because rational doubt is created. Rational doubt is created when the skeptic gives *reasons* for her claim. The reasons are epistemic and pragmatic presuppositions of the skeptic, which contradict the thesis she avers. Therefore, it will not do for the skeptic to claim simply that she *is* justified but cannot justify her claim, because without her giving reasons for her claim there is *no problem*—rational doubt would not have been created—and her claim would carry no epistemological "weight."

There is also a tradition in epistemology of relying on intuitions to justify a variety of different claims not just to oneself, but especially to others, known as reflective equilibrium. When Rawls asks us to put ourselves into the "original position," he is asking us to tap into our intuitions to justify a system of distributive justice. Hence, this does not seem to be a fruitful path for the skeptic to pursue.

So, again we arrive at the conclusion that the skeptic's impossible condition is neither sufficient nor necessary for settling the dispute and justifying a knowledge claim. Furthermore, the skeptic's position is self-defeating because she cannot maintain her thesis without epistemic self-refutation. This is because to maintain the thesis she must provide some reason for the claim. Such reasons will inevitably rely either on the canons of logic or on intuition. In either case, the skeptic thereby admits that there are other ways to justify a knowledge claim (or justified belief claim), thus contradicting the thesis she espouses. If she provides no reason for the claim then her thesis is completely unsupported and creates no problem for methodists and particularists. This is because rational doubt is the earmark of a philosophical problem. The skeptic's claim must be supported by reasons to make it reasonable, even if her reason is only an appeal to intuition. Without such reasons her skeptical claim is not a part of an inconsistent set of individually *reasonable* beliefs. This means that some form of methodism or particularism or mixture of the two (i.e., some form of cognitivism), is more reasonable than *this* form of skepticism.

PYRRHONIAN SKEPTICISM

My antiskeptical argument applies to skeptics who presuppose, pragmatically or epistemically, the principles of logic and/or those who presuppose intuition to maintain their theses. But what about a skeptic who makes no such presuppositions? Could such a skeptic evade my criticisms and still pose the problem of the criterion? Sextus Empiricus is such a skeptic. Since my critique relies on the presuppositions of the skeptic, Pyrrhonian skepticism would be immune to my criticism. The Pyrrhonian skeptic takes no position and makes no presuppositions, epistemic or pragmatic. But, as I discussed in Chapter 2, if Sextus takes no position, then criticism of the standard accepted as necessary to settle the dispute is really a criticism of Stoicism, not Pyrrhonian Skepticism.

If the supporters of Sextus Empiricus are correct about "having a view" (see Chapter 2), then Pyrrhonian Skepticism does present certain difficulties for Stoic epistemology. Could a *modern* Pyrrhonian skeptic present similar kinds of problems for particularists and methodists? The difficulty in answering this question immediately presents itself when we realize that the ancient Pyrrhonian skeptic's "nonassertions" were made in the context of, and in response to, a single epistemology—Stoic epistemology. But there are particularists and methodists of every ilk, representing a wide range of epistemological theories with conflicting theses and presuppositions.

Hence, it seems that we can only answer this question in the abstract. What a modern Pyrrhonian could do is claim (nonassertively) that *given* epistemology X and dispute Y between individuals P, Q, and R, it *seems to him* that settlement is not possible. And if we filled in the variables with constants that included Chisholm's questions (A) and (B) and disputants that were particularists, methodists, and skeptics (modern dogmatic ones), then the Pyrrhonian could claim (again, nonassertively) that settlement was not possible. And, as I stated in Chapter 5, I would agree with the skeptic's assessment, but demonstrate that the "problem" dissolves. The more interesting questions about what is or is not necessary for metajustification are issues that we must raise with the more dogmatic skeptic, because the Pyrrhonian takes no position on this or any other issue. The Pyrrhonian is forever context dependent on those who take positions.

Of course, the Pyrrhonian may have important insights into many other epistemological issues that do not touch directly upon the problem of the criterion. But as far as the problem of the criterion is concerned, the factors that make the Pyrrhonian immune to my criticism also keep him insulated from making a substantial contribution to our discussion of metajustification. Nonetheless, he would be correct in stating what is now obvious, that settlement of the dispute is impossible if settlement requires meeting a condition that is impossible. But that much can also be said of the more dogmatic, modern skeptic of Chisholm and Rescher.

William Alston calls the skeptic's impossible condition "full reflective justification" (FRJ) and claims that it is a pipe dream.[21] While I would concur with Alston here, I believe that the importance of this insight lies in its connection to the skeptic's position. A person who maintains that FRJ is necessary and/or sufficient to settle the dispute, even though FRJ is, in principle, impossible to satisfy, maintains a position that is self-undermining. This makes the skeptic's position less reasonable than either particularism or methodism, which, although also not amenable to FRJ, do not suffer the defect of being self-destructive. Many philosophers, most prominently Chisholm, have realized that they may *be* justified in their epistemological theses, that they may know them to be true, even though they cannot fully reflectively justify their claims.[22]

The impossibility of FRJ need not lead one to relativism or contextualism—the thesis that justification is relative to a context—because although one may not be able to fully reflectively justify any belief, one may still *be* justified in such beliefs and one may know such beliefs to be true.[23] The interesting issue that we are left to deal with concerns how we are to determine the standards by which we discern whether particularists or methodists are correct. This is a meta-metaepistemological issue concerning second order standards of justification. I would like to indicate the direction I think this inquiry should take, although an indication is all I can give here.

METAEPISTEMOLOGY AND STANDARDS

If the *activity* of justification is always relative to some context, then the process of determining what standards of justification are acceptable will occur within a context, within a set of background assumptions and presuppositions. This gives us a reason to think that looking to common assumptions will figure in how we determine such standards. I believe that this is at the heart of Black's insight that a demand for justification is normally taken to imply a discrepancy with some standard, a standard temporarily fixed and accepted by the disputants.[24] If there are common assumptions, will they lead us to one standard? Will they lead us to the best possible standard? What would make one standard better than another? Is there a single standard that *rational* settlement *ought to follow*? These questions open a Pandora's box in epistemology. I shall try to set out a rough outline within which we may begin to address them.

Stich offers some useful distinctions for our purposes, the most important of which is between "descriptive cognitive pluralism" and "normative cognitive pluralism."[25] This distinction is similar to one in ethics between descriptive ethical relativism and normative ethical relativism. Descriptive cognitive pluralism claims that people reason, form, and revise beliefs and other ways of cognizing in importantly different ways. A descriptive cognitive monist would deny that these differences, if any, are significant, and maintain that we all cognize in basically the same way. Normative cognitive pluralism states that there is no one system of cognizing that people *ought* to use, that is the *best* to use. Different, even conflicting, ways of reasoning may all be equally good. The normative cognitive monist would deny this claim and maintain that even if people did reason in significantly different ways, they *should* all reason the same way, the rational way. There are correct ways of reasoning and faulty ways of reasoning, and that is that.

If descriptive cognitive pluralism is true, then it is possible that our disputants share no common assumptions, that they reason in vastly different ways. The empirical evidence for descriptive cognitive pluralism is meager and open to question.[26] But in any case the more significant issue is the normative one. For if normative cognitive pluralism is false, then even if descriptive cognitive pluralism is true, people *ought* to reason in one basic way. And this is the standard that ought to be used to settle disputes about what counts as a rational justification of a knowledge claim. If normative cognitive pluralism is true, then settlement may only be possible where disputants share similar ways of reasoning.[27]

Stich offers a spirited defense of normative cognitive pluralism in the *Fragmentation of Reason* and it may be worth our while to review his basic argument and assess it. Stich's account begins with the empirical findings of psychologists, such as Nisbet, who conclude that people in fact reason badly. This conclusion is based upon the results of experiments, such as the now classic "selection task" of P. N. Johnson-Laird and P. C. Wason shown in Figure 6-1.[28]

In Figure 6–1, which of the hidden parts of these cards do you need to see in order to answer the following question decisively? FOR THESE CARDS, IS IT TRUE THAT IF THERE IS A CIRCLE ON THE LEFT THERE IS A CIRCLE ON THE RIGHT? (You have only one opportunity to make this decision; you must not assume that you can inspect the cards one at a time. Name those cards that it is absolutely essential to see.)

Most university students answer incorrectly. In one group, 123 out of 128 were wrong, most typically with responses of "both (a) and (c)" or "only (a)." Few understood that (d) must also be uncovered. Stich claims that two questions arise from these and similar findings: "What sorts of interventions

Skepticism and the Problem

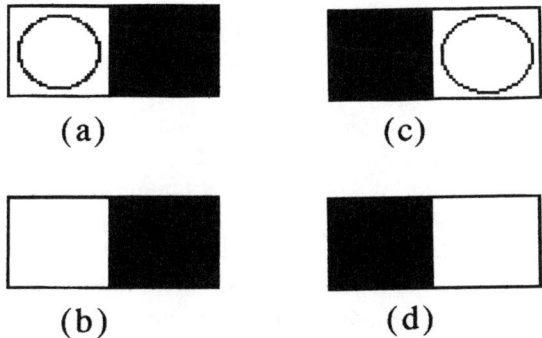

Figure 6-1. *Selection Task*

will succeed in changing the way people go about the business of reasoning?" (an empirical question) and "What sorts of changes would be *desirable*?" (a normative question).[29]

The normative question is the one of most philosophical interest. Stich claims that the two most popular answers to the normative question concern how one's beliefs are related to (1) justification and (2) truth. Most philosophers, including myself, believe that it is desirable, from an epistemic point of view, to change one's beliefs in such a way that one has more justified beliefs than unjustified or more true beliefs than false in a relevantly specified area. Stich presents two similar arguments against these two claims.

Stich prefaces his argument with a thought experiment. Imagine a powerful genie who offers to make one change in the way you reason, acquire beliefs, and revise them. You could wish for more justified beliefs and fewer unjustified (compared to the set you would have without the genie's intervention), or more true beliefs and fewer false, or ones generated by a more reliable cognitive system, and so on. Stich claims that "when we view the matter clearly," most of us will not find the genie's offer tempting.[30] He provides the following argument to support his claim:

1. To find something tempting is to find it more desirable than alternatives.
2. Something is desirable either intrinsically, instrumentally, or both.
3. If X is desirable intrinsically, then X is desirable for its own sake; and if X is desirable instrumentally, then X is desirable for the sake of something else. If X is desirable both intrinsically and instrumentally, then it X is desirable for its own sake and for the sake of something else.
4. If the genie's offer to have more justified beliefs and fewer unjustified ones is desirable, then it is desirable either intrinsically, instrumentally, or both.

5. Our concept of justification is highly idiosyncratic and accidental.

6. Idiosyncratic and accidental justified beliefs are not intrinsically desirable.

7. Therefore, the genie's offer of more justified beliefs and fewer unjutified ones is not intrinsically desirable.

8. Because our concept of justification is highly idiosyncratic, there are many other justificationlike concepts that appear to be just as instrumentally desirable as justification.

9. Therefore, we have no reason to believe that justification is more instrumentally valuable than many other justification-like concepts.

10. Hence, if the genie gave us a choice between more justified beliefs, more JUSTIFIED* beliefs, and more JUSTIFIED** beliefs, we would not find any one alternative more desirable than the others.

11. Therefore, having more justified beliefs would not be more tempting or more desirable, intrinsically or instrumentally, than countless other offers.

Stich's argument against true belief is much the same, substituting truth or true belief wherever justification and justified belief appear. A bit of explanation about why Stich believes that our notions of justification and truth are idiosyncratic will help make the arguments understandable. Stich uses Goldman's analysis of justification to illustrate the idiosyncratic nature of the concept of justification that is embedded in our thought and language.

According to Stich, Goldman seeks to build a theory of justification by explaining the rules that evaluate the justificatory status of our beliefs (J-rules). The J-rules are determined by a higher criterion of rightness. "The correct criterion of rightness is the one that comports with the conception of justifiedness that is embraced by everyday thought and language."[31] But, says Stich, why should we want this? Isn't this conception of justifiedness merely something we have acquired *culturally*? If so, it might vary from culture to culture. And if so, why should we *value* such a criterion on the contingent grounds that it accords with a concept that is culturally based and relative? And on what grounds could we choose between a criterion based on one culture's embedded epistemic conception and another culture's criterion based on their embedded epistemic conception? Hence, our notion of justification is idiosyncratic and accidental.

His case against truth or true belief is slightly more involved. Stich begins by assuming a token identity theory of mind—that belief tokens are identical with brain state tokens. These belief tokens have semantic properties in virtue of the fact that they can be mapped onto propositions. "A belief token is true if it is mapped to a true proposition."[32] Stich explains that our notion of a *true* belief is idiosyncratic because it "results from the idiosyncracy of our intuitive strategy for mapping beliefs to propositions."[33] The idea here is that *some* brain state tokens (i.e., the "intentional" ones) have semantic properties because they are related, via a mapping or interpretation function, to propositions.

Stich invokes the causal/functional theory of interpretation function to explain why our notion of truth or true belief is idiosyncratic. In brief, the causal/functional theory claims that "elaborate causal chains [link] the concepts out of which our beliefs are built to various objects, kinds and classes in the world."[34] As Stich explains:

> Consider, for example, the belief token that I would express by saying "Thales drank water." Our intuitive "interpretation function" maps one component of that belief to a certain ancient sage, and another component to H_2O. Thus the belief is true if and only if that sage drank H_2O. However, there is another function, albeit a counter-intuitive one, that maps the first component of the belief to some other ancient, and still another function that maps the last component to H_2O or XYZ. If we exploit this second, counterintuitive, function then we can define what might be called the TRUTH* condition for the belief token I express by saying "Thales drank water." That belief token is TRUE* if and only if a certain ancient sage drank either H_2O or XYZ.[35]

Once we see how idiosyncratic our notion of truth or true belief really is, one can see why, argues Stich, having true beliefs is neither intrinsically valuable nor instrumentally superior to a host of other notions we could adopt, such as TRUE* beliefs or TRUE** beliefs. Stich proposes a pragmatic theory to evaluate and choose between alternative systems. We need not get into the details of that theory here.

Both Goldman and Harman criticize Stich for confusing truth with interpretation function.[36] There is only one rival to truth, and that is falsity. TRUTH* and TRUTH** are not truth values, but rather amalgamations of interpretation functions and truth values. Truth is simple. If I believe that my dog Bear is sleeping, then my belief is true if and only if my dog Bear is sleeping. Stich's charge of idiosyncracy applies not to our notion of truth, but to the interpretation function we intuitively accept. And so, Stich's argument does not show that truth is not intrinsically or instrumentally valuable, but that there are a variety of interpretation functions in addition to the one we intuitively accept; and, Stich would argue, we have no reason to prefer our interpretation function over others.

As Goldman explains: "Once we learn about alternative I.F.s, why should we value being in brain states that turn out true on the ordinary I.F. (true beliefs) rather than brain states that turn out true on some non-standard I.F. (true BELIEFS*)?"[37] Goldman offers two answers to this question: (1) that nonstandard interpretation functions may not link up with actions in helpful ways; and (2) for those that do, we can recognize their value as well, without rejecting our own. If we need to make a choice in some case, Goldman opts for its link to action as the best criterion of choice. After all, we value true beliefs not only because we are wonderers by nature, but also because true beliefs are instrumentally useful in achieving desired goals.

In conclusion, Stich has not demonstrated that justification and truth are idiosyncratic, or that they are not intrinsically or instrumentally valuable. Since justified beliefs are valued epistemically because of their connection with truth, justified beliefs would have at least instrumental value. Hence, he has not shown that normative cognitive pluralism is true. If I were faced with Stich's genie, I would find more justified or more true beliefs quite tempting.

With the specter of normative cognitive pluralism in abeyance, we may hope for a second order standard for justification through mutually accepted principles based on a common desire to justify systems that aim at truth. If our disputants can agree upon a set of metastandards, perhaps based upon shared epistemological goals, these principles may be sufficiently restrictive to create a second order standard for the *activity* of justification. If particularist or methodist or skeptic *is justified* in his claim, then perhaps he can use this belief to fashion standards for acceptable acts of justifying such a belief. But such standards will have to avoid circularity and be ones that are mutually acceptable to all parties.

One way to start, then, would be to take our principle of justification (JP) seriously. Recall what it states:

> JP: If S *is* justified in believing that P at least partially on the basis of Q, and S believes that S is justified in believing that P at least partially on the basis of Q, and Q is an epistemic presupposition of P for S, then S accepts Q as a means of at least partially justifying S's belief that P.

Since each disputant believes himself to *be* justified in his claims, each accepts something other than a justification-by-argument as an organon for conferring epistemic merit. The disputants each have a reason to move toward a new metastandard, guided by (JP), as it applies to their beliefs about first order knowledge claims. If they could agree on this organon, progress would have been made toward an acceptable process of justifying first order knowledge claims. However, the same organon will not guarantee settlement of their dispute. But it is a necessary first step. As we noted earlier, intuition is a candidate, but there are others as well—perhaps introspection or memory or perception or coherence or even an infinite justificatory chain that makes reference to its successor.

Ernest Sosa outlines a similar suggestion when he claims that we may need to replace or demote our notion of justification-as-an-argument and favor a more appropriate term such as "apt" belief.[38] Apt belief is a belief with the positive epistemic merit necessary for knowledge, but it is acquired without an argumentative justifying process or activity. By virtue of its *satisfying* certain conditions, it acquires epistemic merit. If our disputants can agree on what constitutes such apt belief, perhaps partially in terms of their own claims to knowledge, then settlement of their disagreement will be possible. There may also be certain fundamental metaprinciples, that, when combined with the accepted organon, would aid in selecting a first order system. Such principles might look like the following:

1. Metacriteria and criteria should be consistent with the law of noncontradiction and should yield beliefs that are not inconsistent.
2. All other things being equal, criteria and metacriteria with greater explanatory power should be preferred.
3. A metacriterion should apply to itself, that is, it should be knowable by its own principle.

However, if we had agreement on these principles, without agreement on the organon, I suspect that these principles would not be specific enough to rule out various forms of methodism, particularism, and skepticism. Yet more specific principles would be likely to spawn disagreement among our disputants. Settlement seems to rest upon their ability to agree on the organon. If we find that the skeptic, methodist, and particularist cannot come to an agreement on this third order question, then we may be at an impasse in our dialogue—at least concerning the issue of the *activity* of justification and the possibility of settling their dispute. If this is so, it seems to me preferable to be clear that we disagree at some absolutely fundamental level, what Robert Fogelin calls a "deep disagreement,"[39] than to mistakenly think that we are caught in a circle of someone else's making or that skepticism is on an equal footing with methodism and particularism. After all, inability to actively justify metacriteria does not impugn the justifiedness of first order knowledge claims by either particularist or methodist. Only the metaepistemological skeptic's position has been undermined.

NOTES

Part of this chapter is reprinted, with changes, from my paper "Skepticism and the Problem of the Criterion," in *On Knowing and the Known*, ed. Ken Lucey (Amherst, N.Y.: Prometheus, 1993), with the permission of the publisher.

1. My thanks to Stewart Cohen for this insight.
2. Rescher seems to interpret the skeptic in this way in *Methodological Pragmatism*, 17 and 97.
3. Richard Fumerton, "Meta-Epistemology and Skepticism." Paper presented at the University of Rochester 6th Annual Conference—Skepticism, May 5–6, 1989, now published in *Doubting*, eds. M. Roth and G. Ross (Dordrecht, Holland: Kluwer, 1990), 57–68.
4. Scott Soames, "Presupposition," in *Handbook of Philosophical Logic*, 553–616.
5. For a thorough and clear account of contextual implication, see Isabel C. Hungerland, "Contextual Implication," *Inquiry* 4 (1960): 211–58.
6. P. F. Strawson, *Introduction to Logical Theory* (London: Methuen, 1952), 175.
7. David Rynin has demonstrated that Strawson's account entails that all presupposed statements are true: $S > S'$; also not-$S > S'$; but $S \vee$ not-S; therefore S'. (See Hungerland, "Contextual Implication," 239.)
8. For the details of this account and its critique, see Soames, 556–60.
9. Stalnaker, "Pragmatics," 180.
10. Hungerland, "Contextual Implication," 239.
11. Sextus Empiricus, PH I.114.
12. See Haack, "Justification of Deduction," 112–19; Amico, "Vindication of Deduction and Induction," 322–30. William Alston refers to deductive and inductive reasoning, as well as sense perception, memory, and introspection as "epistemologically basic sources of belief," which he defines as "O is an (epistemologically) basic source of belief = def. Any (otherwise) cogent argumant for the reliability of O will use premises drawn from O." (See Alston, "Epistemic Circularity," 326.)
13. Black, 63.
14. Pollock, 317–27.
15. This is Haack's appellative for the invalid rule: If P then Q, and Q, therefore P. (See Haack, "Justification of Deduction," 115.)
16. Lewis Carroll, "What the Tortoise Said to Achilles," in *The Complete Works of Lewis Carroll*, 1104–8. (London: Nonesuch Press, 1939); and Rudolf Carnap, "Inductive Logic and Inductive Intuition," in *The Problem of Inductive Logic*, ed. I. Lakatos (Amsterdam: North Holland, 1968).
17. See Chapter 2.
18. Because I have characterized problems in terms of presuppositions, a skeptic cannot hide behind such a tactic. Furthermore, if the skeptic claims that he/she makes no presuppositions in making his/her claim, then not only would his/her claim pose no problem for me, but there would be no way of determining what kind of answer would count as acceptable—the parameters for an acceptable answer are not available. This would make it a pseudoproblem. (See Chapter 1.)
19. My thanks to Sharon Ryan for this point.
20. Alston exploits this distinction interestingly in "Epistemic Circularity," to avoid circularity in justifying an epistemic principle.
21. Alston, "Epistemic Circularity," 349.

22. James Van Cleve makes a similar point in "Foundationalism, Epistemic Principles, and the Cartesian Circle," *Philosophical Review* 88, no. 1 (Jan. 1979): 89.

23. Alston explains contextualism thus:

> [A]ll justification must take place in a context defined by the assumption of certain beliefs that are, in that context, fixed, not subject to question. These beliefs can be questioned in turn, but only in some other context that is defined by some other (temporarily) fixed assumption. For contextualism the attempt to justify our belief system as a whole is quixotic."

Alston, like myself, *only* concurs with the contextualist claim that FRJ is impossible. (See "Epistemic Circularity," 346–49.

24. Black, 63.

25. Stephen Stich, *Fragmentation of Reason*, 13–14.

26. This point is made by Goldman in "Stephen P. Stich: *The Fragmentation of Reason*" *[Philosophy and Phenomenological Research* 51, no. 1 (March 1991): 189], who notes that even Stich admits the evidence is only a "hint" that descriptive cognitive pluralism is true. (See Stich, 166, note 28.)

27. Chisholm makes a similar point in *Foundations of Knowing*, 120–21. He adds: "If they do not share any assumptions or principles, they may yet be able to agree what each of them, given his own assumptions, is justified in thinking that he knows."

28. See P. N. Johnson-Laird and P. C. Wason, "A Theoretical Analysis of Insight into a Reasoning Task," in *Thinking*, ed. P. N. Johnson-Laird and P. C. Wason (Cambridge: Cambridge University Press, 1970).

29. Stephen Stich, "*The Fragmentation of Reason*: Précis of Two Chapters," *Philosophy and Phenomenological Research* 51, no. 1 (March 1991): 179.

30. Ibid., 180.

31. Stich, *Fragmentation of Reason*, 90, who cites Alvin Goldman, *Epistemology and Cognition* (Cambridge: Harvard University Press, 1986), 58–59.

32. Stich, "*Fragmentation of Reason*: Précis of Two Chapters," 182.

33. Ibid.

34. Ibid.

35. Ibid.

36. Goldman, "Stephen P. Stich: *The Fragmentation of Reason*," 189–93; and Gilbert Harman, "Justification, Truth, Goals, and Pragmatism: Comments on Stich's *Fragmentation of Reason*," *Philosophy and Phenomenological Research* 51, no. 1 (March 1991): 195–99.

37. Ibid., 191.

38. Ernest Sosa, "Methodology and Apt Belief," *Synthese* 74 (1988): 415–26; also "Beyond Skepticism, to the Best of Our Knowledge," *Mind* 97, (1988): sect. B4.

39. Robert J. Fogelin, "The Logic of Deep Disagreements," *Informal* Logic 7, no. 1 (1985): 1–8. Fogelin describes a deep disagreement as the result of a clash in underlying principles or framework propositions (or what Wittgenstein called rules), and for which, he believes, no rational resolution is possible.

Chapter 7

Conclusion

We have discovered that the problem of the criterion is a metaepistemological problem concerning the justification of first order knowledge claims among disagreeing disputants. Historically, there have been various characterizations of the problem and not all of them discuss the exact same problem. The various characterizations can be categorized into two main groups—the ancient problem and the modern problem. They differ in terms of their presuppositions, which partially individuate and identify them.

Both problems have a dissolution because, in each case, the condition required for solution is, in principle, impossible to meet. These dissolutions lead to a critique of modern skepticism based upon the self-defeating nature of the modern skeptic's position. Metaepistemic skepticism is shown to be epistemically self-refuting and, hence, much less reasonable than cognitivist positions of either the particularist or methodist persuasion. While the ancient skeptic (Pyrrhonian) is immune to this criticism because he takes no position (and hence cannot have a self-defeating position), this feature of his "view" also forever keeps his context dependent upon those who do take positions, and consequently insulates him from making a substantive contribution to the discussion of metajustification.

Settlement of the dispute is possible, it is argued, only if agreement on the metastandard for acceptable justifications is reached by the disputants. An outline of an approach toward settlement is given in terms of a principle of justification, whereby each disputant admits as an acceptable metastandard that organon that the disputant takes to justify him in his first order knowledge claims. This strategy relies on a distinction between *being* justified and the *activity* of justify*ing* one's beliefs. If agreement can be reached by this maneuver, then settlement may be possible based upon the newly accepted organon. If no agreement is reached, then settlement will not be possible and a justify*ing* of one's first order knowledge claims will not be possible. This is because, as Max Black understood nearly fifty years ago, "'justification' is a relational notion, whose exact specification varies with the type of *standard* of justification to which appeal is to be made."[1] But even if we fail in this

143

task, our failure is not epistemological defeat because inability to actively justify a system makes us no less justified in accepting it.

This conclusion also implies that many of the proposed approaches to solving the problem of the criterion that were rejected as *solutions* to the problem of the criterion—Rescher's methodological pragmatism, Chisholm's particularism, Moser's reflective equilibrium, and even Cardinal Mercier's metacriterion—are all candidates for consideration as metaepistemic approaches to the justification of knowledge claims. Metaepistemology proceeds without the specter of metaepistemic skepticism.

NOTE

1. Black, 61.

Bibliography

Agre, Gene. "The Concept of Problem." *Educational Studies* 13 (1982): 121–41.

———. "What Does It Mean to Solve Problems?" *Journal of Thought* 18 (1983): 92–104.

Alston, William. "Varieties of Privileged Access." *American Philosophical Quarterly* 18 (1971): 223–41.

———. "Epistemic Circularity." *Philosophy and Phenomenological Research* 47 (1986): 1–30.

———. *Epistemic Justification*. Ithaca, N.Y.: Cornell University Press, 1989.

Amico, Robert P. "On the Vindication of Deduction and Induction." *Australasian Journal of Philosophy* 64, no. 3 (1986): 322–30.

———. "Roderick Chisholm and the Problem of the Criterion." *Philosophical Papers* 17, no. 3 (1988): 217–29.

———. "Reply to Chisholm on the Problem of the Criterion." *Philosophical Papers* 17, no. 3 (1988): 235–36.

———. "Skepticism and the Problem of the Criterion." Forthcoming in *On Knowing And The Known*. Edited by Ken Lucey. Amherst, N.Y.: Prometheus, 1993.

Aristotle. *Problemata*. Translated by E. S. Forester. In *The Works of Aristotle*, Vol. 7. Edited by W. D. Ross. Oxford: Clarendon Press, 1927.

———. *Topics*. In *The Basic Works of Aristotle*. Edited by R. McKeon. New York: Random House, 1941.

Audi, R. "Foundationalism and Epistemic Dependence." *Journal of Philosophy* 77, no. 10 (1980): 612–13.

Aune, Bruce. "Remarks on Argument by Chisholm." *Philosophical Studies* 23 (1972): 327–34.

Bailey, A. "Pyrrhonian Scepticism and the Self-Refutation Argument." *Philosophical Quarterly* 40 (Jan. 1990): 27–44.

Barnes, Jonathan. "The Beliefs of a Pyrrhonist." *Proceedings of the Cambridge Philological Society* 208 (1982): 1–29.

Black, Max. *Language and Philosophy*. Ithaca, N.Y.: Cornell University Press, 1949.

Blanchard, Brand. *The Nature of Thought*. 4th Ed.. London: Allen & Unwin, 1964.

Bonjour, Lawrence. "The Coherence Theory of Empirical Knowledge." *Philosophical Studies* 30 (1976): 281–312.

———. "Rescher's Epistemological System." In *The Philosophy of Nicholas Rescher.* Edited by E. Sosa, 157–72. Dordrecht, Holland: Reidel, 1979.

———. *The Structure of Empirical Knowledge.* Cambridge: Harvard University Press, 1985.

Bradley, F. H. *Appearance and Reality.* Oxford: Oxford University Press, 1893.

Broad, C. D. "Mr. Bradley on Truth and Reality." *Mind* 23 (1914): 349–70.

Brown, Harold I. "Paradigmatic Propositions." *American Philosophical Quarterly* 12, no. 1 (1975): 85–90.

———. "Problem Changes in Science and Philosophy." *Metaphilosophy* 6, no. 2 (1975): 177–92.

Burnyeat, Myles. "Protagoras and Self-Refutation in Later Greek Philosophy." *Philosophical Review* 85 (Jan. 1976): 44–69.

———. "Can the Skeptic Live His Skepticism?" In *Doubt and Dogmatism.* Edited by M. Schonfield, M. Burnyeat, and J. Barnes, 20–53. Oxford: Clarendon Press, 1980.

———. "Idealism and Greek Philosophy: What Descartes Saw and Berkeley Missed." *Philosophical Review* 91, no. 1 (Jan. 1982): 3–40.

Campbell, Keith. *Body and Mind.* 2d Ed. Notre Dame: University of Notre Dame Press, 1984.

Carnap, Rudolf. "Inductive Logic and Inductive Intuition." In *The Problem of Inductive Logic.* Edited by I. Lakatos, 258–267. Amsterdam: North-Holland, 1968.

Carroll, Lewis. "What the Tortoise Said to Achilles." In *The Complete Works of Lewis Carroll.* With an introduction by A. Woollcott, 1104–8. London: Nonesuch, 1939.

Chisholm, Roderick M. *Perceiving: A Philosophical Study.* Ithaca, N.Y.: Cornell University Press, 1957.

———. "The Myth of the Given." In *Philosophy.* Edited by R. M. Chisholm, H. Feigl, W. Frankena, J. Passmore, and M. Thompson, 261–86. Englewood Cliffs: Prentice-Hall, 1964.

———. *The Problem of the Criterion.* Milwaukee, Wis.: Marquette University Press, 1973.

———. *The Foundations of Knowing.* Minneapolis: University of Minnesota Press, 1982.

———. "The Indispensability of Internal Justification." *Synthese* 74 (1988): 285–96.

———. "Reply to Amico on the Problem of the Criterion."*Philosophical Papers* 17, no. 3 (Nov. 1988): 231–34.

———. *Theory of Knowledge.* Englewood Cliffs, N.J.: Prentice-Hall, 2d ed., 1977; 3d Ed., 1989.

———. "The Status of Epistemic Principles." *Nous* 24 (1990): 209–15.
Cicero. *Academia*. Edited by J. S. Reid. London: Macmillan, 1885.
Coffey, P. *Epistemology or Theory of Knowledge*. 2 vols. London: Longmans, Green, 1917.
Cohen, L. Jonathan. "Can Human Irrationality Be Experimentally Demonstrated?" *Behavioral and Brain Sciences* 4 (1981): 317–31.
Cornman, J. *Skepticism, Justification and Explanation*. Dordrecht, Holland: Reidel, 1980.
Current State of the Coherence Theory. Edited by J. W. Bender. Dordrecht, Holland: Kluwer, 1989.
Deichegraber, Karl. *Die Greichische Empirikerschule*. Berlin: Weidmann, 1930.
DePaul, Michael. "Reflective Equilibrium and Foundationalism." *American Philosophical Quarterly* 23, no. 1 (1986): 59–69.
Dewey, John. *How We Think*. Boston: Heath, 1910.
Diogenes Laertius. *Lives of Eminent Philosophers*. 2 vols. Translated by R. D. Hicks. Cambridge: Harvard University Press, 1925.
Epistemology: New Essays in the Theory of Knowledge. Edited by Avrum Stroll. New York: Harper and Row, 1967.
Essays on Knowledge and Justification. Edited by George Pappas and Marshall Swain. Ithaca, N.Y.: Cornell University Press, 1978.
Feldman, Richard. "Fallibilism and Knowing That One Knows." *Philosophical Review* 90 (1981): 266–82.
Firth, Roderick. "Coherence, Certainty and Epistemic Priority." *Journal of Philosophy* 61 (1964): 545–57.
Fogelin, Robert J. "The Logic of Deep Disagreements." *Informal Logic* 7, no. 1 (1985): 1–8.
Foley, R. "Inferential Justification and the Infinite Regress." *American Philosophical Quarterly* 15, no. 4 (1978): 311–16.
Frede, Michael. "Review of *Greek Skepticism*." *Journal of Philosophy* 70 (1973): 805–10.
———. "Stoics and Skeptics on Clear and Distinct Impressions." In *The Skeptical Tradition*. Edited by Myles Burnyeat, 65–94. Berkeley: University of California Press, 1983.
———. *Essays in Ancient Philosophy*. Minneapolis: University of Minnesota Press, 1987.
Fumerton, Richard. "Meta-Epistemology and Scepticism." In *Doubting*. Edited by M. Roth and G. Ross, 57–68. Dordrecht, Holland: Kluwer, 1990.
Ginet, C. *Knowledge, Memory and Perception*. Dordrecht, Holland: Reidel, 1975.
Goldman, A. *Epistemology and Cognition*. Cambridge: Harvard University Press, 1986.

———. "Stephen P. Stich: *The Fragmentation of Reason.*" *Philosophy and Phenomenological Research* 51, no. 1 (March 1991): 189–93.

Goodman, Nelson. *Fact, Fiction and Forecast.* Cambridge: Harvard University Press, 1955.

Haack, Susan. "The Justification of Deduction." *Mind* 85 (Jan. 1976): 112–19.

———. "Theories of Knowledge: An Analytic Framework." *Proceedings of the Aristotelian Society* 83 (1982–83): 143–57.

Hallie, P. *Skepticism, Man and God.* Middletown, Conn.: Wesleyan University Press, 1964.

Hanson, N. R. *Patterns of Discovery.* Cambridge: Cambridge University Press, 1958.

Harker, J. "Can There Be an Infinite Regress of Justified Beliefs?" *Australasian Journal of Philosophy* 62, no. 3 (1984): 255–64.

Harman, Gilbert. *Thought.* Princeton, N.J.: Princeton University Press, 1973.

———. "Justification, Truth, Goals and Pragmatism: Comments on Stich's *Fragmentation of Reason.*" *Philosophy and Phenomenological Research* 51, no. 1 (March 1991): 195–99.

Hattiangadi, J. N. "The Structure of Problems, Part I." *Philosophy of the Social Sciences* 8 (1978): 345–65.

———. "The Structure of Problems, Part II." *Philosophy of the Social Sciences* 9 (1979): 49–76.

Hellenistic Philosophy: Introductory Readings. Translated by B. Inwood and L. P. Gerson. Indianapolis: Hackett, 1988.

Hungerland, Isabel C. "Contextual Implication." *Inquiry* 4 (1960): 211–58.

Johnson-Laird, P. N., and P. C. Wason. "A Theoretical Analysis of Insight into a Reasoning Task." In *Thinking.* Edited by P. N. Johnson-Laird and P. C. Wason, 143–57. Cambridge: Cambridge University Press, 1970.

Kneale, W., and M. Kneale. *The Development of Logic.* Oxford: Clarendon Press, 1962.

Kornblith, Hilary. "Beyond Foundationalism and the Coherence Theory." *Journal of Philosophy* 77, no. 10 (1980): 597–612.

Lehe, Robert. "Coherence and the Problem of the Criterion." *Idealistic Studies* 19, no. 2 (1989): 112–20.

Lehrer, Keith. *Knowledge.* Oxford: Oxford University Press, 1974.

———. "Reply to My Critics." In *Current State of the Coherence Theory.* Edited by John Bender, 258–59. Dordrecht, Holland: Kluwer, 1989.

Lemos, Noah. "Coherence and Epistemic Priority." *Philosophical Studies* 41 (1982): 299–315.

Long, A. A. *Hellenistic Philosophy.* London: G. Duckworth, 1974.

Lucey, Ken. *On Knowing and the Known.* Amherst, N.Y.: Prometheus, 1993.

Mackie, J. L. "Self-Refutation—A Formal Analysis." *Philosophical Quarterly* 14, no. 56 (July 1964): 193–203.

McPherran, Mark L. "Skeptical Homeopathy and Self-refutation." *Phronesis* 32 (1987): 290–328.

Mates, Benson. *Stoic Logic*. Berkeley: University of California Press, 1973.

Mercier, D. J. *Criteriologie*. 8th Ed. Paris: Felix Alcan, 1923.

———. *A Manual of Modern Scholastic Philosophy*. Translated by T. L. Parker and S. A. Parker. London: Kegan Paul, Trench, Trubner, 1928.

Montaigne, Michael de. "Apology for Raymond Sebond." In *Essays of Michael de Montaigne*. Translated and edited by Jacob Zeitlin. New York: Knopf, 1935.

———. "Apology for Raymond Sebond." In *Essays of Michael de Montaigne*. Translated by E. Trenchmann. New York: Modern Library, 1946.

Moser, Paul. *Knowledge and Evidence*. Cambridge: Cambridge University Press, 1989.

———. "Lehrer's Coherentism and the Isolation Objection." In *Current State of the Coherence Theory*. Edited by John Bender, 29–37. Dordrecht, Holland: Kluwer, 1989.

Naess, Arne. *Skepticism*. New York: Humanities, 1968.

Owen, John. *The Skeptics of the French Renaissance*. London: Swan, Sonnenschein, 1893.

Philosophical Problems and Arguments: An Introduction. 3d Ed. Edited by J. Cornman, K. Lehrer, and G. Pappas. New York: Macmillan, 1982.

Philosophical Works of Descartes. Translated by E. Haldane and G. R. T. Ross. Cambridge: Cambridge University Press, 1967.

Plato. *Apology*. In *The Collected Dialogues of Plato*. Edited by Edith Hamilton. Princeton, N.J.: Princeton University Press, 1961.

———. *Meno*. 2d. ed. Translated by G. M. A. Grube. Indianapolis: Hackett, 1981.

Pollock, J. *Knowledge and Justification*. Princeton, N.J.: Princeton University Press, 1974.

Popkin, R. H. *The History of Skepticism from Erasmus to Spinoza*. Berkeley: University of California Press, 1979.

Post, J. F. "Infinite Regresses of Justification and of Explanation." *Philosophical Studies* 38 (1980): 31–52.

Price, Richard. *Review of the Principle Questions of Morals*. Edited by D. Daiches Raphael. Oxford: Clarendon Press, 1948.

Problem of Abortion. Edited by Joel Feinberg. Belmont, Calif.: Wadsworth, 1984.

Quine, W. V. "Truth by Convention." In *The Ways of Paradox and Other Essays*, 77–106. Cambridge: Cambridge University Press, 1966.

———. *The Web of Belief*. New York: Random House, 1970.

Readings in Philosophical Analysis. Edited by H. Feigl and W. Sellars. New York: Appleton-Century-Crofts, 1949.

Rescher, Nicholas. *The Coherence Theory of Truth.* Oxford: Clarendon Press, 1973

———. *The Primacy of Practice.* Oxford: Basil Blackwell, 1973.

———. *Methodological Pragmatism.* Oxford: Basil Blackwell, 1977.

———. "Philosophical Disagreement: An Essay Towards Orientational Pluralism in Metaphilosophy." *Review of Metaphysics* 32 (1978): 217–51.

———. "Reply to Bonjour." In *The Philosophy of Nicholas Rescher.* Edited by E. Sosa, 173–74. Dordrecht, Holland: Reidel, 1979.

———. *Scepticism.* Totowa, N.J.: Rowman & Littlefield, 1980.

———. *The Strife of Systems, An Essay on the Grounds and Implications of Philosophical Diversity.* Pittsburgh, Penn.: University of Pittsburgh Press, 1985.

———. *Rationality.* Oxford: Clarendon Press, 1988.

Resnick, L. "Some Doubts about Skepticism." *Philosophia* 17 (1987): 141–48.

Rist, J. M. *Stoic Philosophy.* Cambridge: Cambridge University Press, 1969.

Russell, Bertrand. *The Problems of Philosophy.* Oxford: Oxford University Press, 1912.

Ryan, Sharon. "Reply to Amico on Skepticism and the Problem of the Criterion." Forthcoming in *On Knowing and the Known.* Edited by Ken Lucey. Amherst, N.Y.: Prometheus, 1993.

Salmon, W. C. *The Foundations of Scientific Inference.* Pittsburgh, Penn.: University of Pittsburgh Press, 1966.

Sandbach, F. H. "Phantasia Kataleptike." In *Problems in Stoicism.* Edited by A. A. Long, 9–21. London: Athlone Press, 1971.

Sellars, Wilfred. "Empiricism and the Philosophy of Mind." In *Science, Perception and Reality*, 127–96. London: Routledge & Kegan Paul, 1963.

Sextus Empiricus. 4 vols. Translated and edited by R. G. Bury. Cambridge: Harvard University Press, 1935.

Skeptical Tradition. Edited by Myles Burnyeat. Berkeley: University of California Press, 1983.

Smullyan, Raymond. *The Lady or the Tiger?* New York: Knopf, 1983.

Soames, Scott. "Presupposition." In *Handbook of Philosophical Logic*, 553–616. Vol. 4. Dordrecht, Holland: Reidel, 1989.

Sosa, E. "Foundations of Foundationalism." *Nous* 4 (Nov. 1980): 547–64.

———. "The Raft and the Pyramid." In *Midwest Studies in Philosophy*, vol. 5. Edited by P. French, T. Uehling, and H. Wettstein, 3–25. Minneapolis: University of Minnesota Press, 1980.

———. "The Coherence of Virtue and the Virtue of Coherence." *Synthese* 64 (1985): 3–28.

———. "Methodology and Apt Belief." *Synthese* 74 (1988): 415–26.

———. "Beyond Skepticism, to the Best of Our Knowledge." *Mind* 97 (1988): 153–88.

Stalnaker, Robert. "Presuppositions." *Journal of Philosophical Logic* 2 (1973): 447–57.

———. "Pragmatic Presuppositions." In *Semantics and Philosophy*. Edited by M. Munitz and P. Unger, 197–213. New York: New York University Press, 1974.

———. "Pragmatics." In *The Philosophy of Language*. 2d Ed. Edited by A. P. Martinich, 176–186. New York: Oxford University Press, 1990.

Steup, Mathias. "The Regress of Metajustification." *Philosophical Studies* 55 (1989): 41–56.

———. "Particularism and the Justification of Epistemic Principles." Unpublished manuscript.

Stich, Stephen. "Reflective Equilibrium, Analytic Epistemology and the Problem of Cognitive Diversity." *Synthese* 74 (1988): 391–413.

———. *The Fragmentation of Reason*. Cambridge: MIT Press, 1990.

———. "*The Fragmentation of Reason*: Précis of Two Chapters." *Philosophy and Phenomenological Research* 51, no. 1 (March 1991): 179–83.

Stoicorum Veterum Fragmenta. Vol. 2. Edited by H. von Arnim. Stuttgart: Teubner, 1964.

Stough, Charlotte L. *Greek Skepticism*. Berkeley: University of California Press, 1969.

———. "Sextus Empiricus on Non-Assertion." *Phronesis* 29 (1984): 137–64.

Strawson, P. F. *Introduction to Logical Theory*. London: Methuen, 1952.

Striker, G. "Skeptical Strategies." In *Doubt and Dogmatism*. Edited by M. Schonfield, M. Burnyeat, and J. Barnes, 54–83. Oxford: Clarendon Press, 1980.

Van Cleve, James. "Foundationalism, Epistemic Principles and the Cartesian Circle." *Philosophical Review* 88, no. 1 (Jan. 1979): 55–91.

Vlastos, Gregory. "Socrates' Disavowal of Knowledge." *Philosophical Quarterly* 35, no. 138 (Jan. 1985): 1–31.

Will, F. L. *Induction and Justification*. Ithaca, N.Y.: Cornell University Press, 1974.

Williams, Michael. *Groundless Belief*. Oxford: Basil Blackwell, 1977.

———. "Scepticism without Theory." *Review of Metaphysics* 41 (March 1988): 547–88.

Index

Agre, Gene, 4
Alston, William, 104, 133
Amico, Robert, 113, 115n
appearance. *See* impression, Sextus on
apt belief, 139
Aristotle, 7, 64, 83, 103
Augustine, St., 27
Aune, Bruce, 105

beg the question. *See* circular reasoning
Black, Max, 108, 111, 124, 134, 143
Bonjour, Laurence, 71n
Bradley, Francis H., 101, 102
Broad, Charlie, D., 102
Brown, Harold I., 5, 8, 13
Burnyeat, Myles, 34; on self-refutation, 31–33, 37, 127

Carnap, Rudolf, 125
Carroll, Lewis, 125
Cartesian. *See* Descartes, René
Chisholm, Roderick M., 1, 3, 61, 93, 106, 120, 144; and coherentism, 98, 99, 102; and the problem of the criterion, 73–89, 111–113; definition of withholding a proposition, 9; on interpreting Sextus Empiricus, 107; on reviving the problem, 2, 43, 102; on skepticism, 119, 126; on the infinite regress, 103, 105
circularity. *See* circular reasoning
circular reasoning, 3, 17, 18, 36, 39, 43, 62, 68, 73, 80, 83–85, 88, 89, 100, 106, 138; and coherence, 101, 102; premise, 101; rule, 101, 102; vicious, 19, 100, 101, 103, 110
Coffey, Peter, 2, 49, 61, 75
cognitive impression. *See* impression, Stoics on
Cohen, Stewart, 140n
coherence theory of justification, 74, 93, 94, 96–99, 105, 119; and circularity, 101; and epistemic dependence, 98, 99; and epistemic priority, 98, 99; and laws of logic, 102; and reflective equilibrium, 99–101; and Rescher's system, 66, 68; as organon, 139; radical, 94, 95, 97, 104
coherentism. *See* coherence theory of justification
coherence theory of truth, 66
Copleston, F. C., 8

Descartes, René, 1, 27, 75, 77
Dewey, John, 4
dissolution of a problem: definition of, 13, 106; of ancient problem of

the criterion, 110–111, 143; of modern problem of the criterion, 113, 114, 126, 143
dogmatic skepticism. *See* skeptic, dogmatic

epistemic dependence, 97, 99, 100, 119; definition of, 98;
epistemic presupposition. *See* presupposition, epistemic
epistemic priority, 23, 98–100, 104, 119; principle of, 74; Roderick Firth's account of, 97
epistemic self-refutation. *See* self-refutation, epistemic
equipollence, Sextus's account of, 25, 26, 29–30, 32–36, 106–107

Feldman, Richard, 90n, 91n
Frede, Michael, 22, 25, 32, 33
Frege, Gottlob, 121
firm assent. *See* irrefutable provability
Firth, Roderick, 97
Fogelin, Robert, 139
foundationalism, 23, 66, 93, 103, 105; epistemic, 94; formal, 93, 94; metaepistemic, 94, 98; substantive, 93, 94, 97
Fumerton, Richard, 120

Goldman, Alvin, 136, 137, 138
Goodman, Nelson, 99

Haack, Susan, 100
Harker, Jay, 104
Harman, Gilbert, 137
Hattiangadi, J. N., 4
Hume, David, 77, 78
Hungerland, Isabel, 121, 122

impression, 18–20, 35, 36; Mercier on, 43; Montaigne on, 40–42; Sextus on, 26–28, 32, 34, 36–38, 69, 87, 106–110; Stoics on, 21–25, 36
infinite regress, 17, 19, 36, 39, 44, 62, 75, 101, 110; argument against foundationalism, 93; of justification, 103–106
intuition, 41, 100, 123, 128–129, 138; and laws of logic, 124–126; justification by, 130–132, 139; problems as conflicting, 7
intuitionism: methodological, 96–98; particular, 96–98
irrefutable provability, 44, 45, 49; in Sextus's argument, 35–37, 41; Stoic thesis of, defined, 24; Stoicism and, 28–30, 87, 107–111

Johnson-Laird, P. N., 134
justification, 93, 94, 108, 111, 122, 134, 139, 143; and Mercier, 44, 45, 47–50; and normative cognitive pluralism, 135–138; and the modern problem of the criterion, 112–114; for deductive logic, 123–126; from the skeptic, 119, 121, 127–131; full reflective, 133; principle of, 127, 138; Rescher's pragmatic, 62–68, 112
justification by coherence. *See* coherence theory of justification

Kneale, W., and Kneale, M., 33

Lehe, Robert, 102
Locke, John, 77
logical paradox, 10
Long, A. A., 22, 24

Mercier, Cardinal D. J., 2, 14, 43–50, 61, 74, 75, 144
metacriterion, 101, 139, 140, 144; Mercier's, 45–47, 74, 75
methodism, 77, 87–89, 94–99, 103, 105, 112–114, 119, 124, 125, 127–133, 138–140, 143; Chisholm's objections to, 78–80; coherence as a form of, 100; defense of, 81–86
methodological pragmatism. *See* justification, Rescher's pragmatic
Montaigne, Michael de, 2, 14, 38–45, 48, 61, 62, 73, 74, 87
Moore, George E., 76, 78
Moser, Paul, 15n17, 67, 99–101, 107, 119, 144

particularism, 76, 94–100, 103, 105, 119, 124, 125, 127–130, 132, 133, 138–140, 143; and the modern problem, 112–114; Chisholm and, 80–89
pluralism: descriptive cognitive, 134; normative cognitive, 134, 138
Pollock, J., 104, 125
Popkin, R. H., 41
presupposition, 8, 11, 43, 50, 103, 109, 111, 143; epistemic, 122–124, 126, 127, 129–132; pragmatic, 5, 9, 12, 76, 77, 88, 89, 122–124, 126, 129–132; the skeptic's, 119–122
problem, 3; identity conditions for, 11; nature of, 6–10; philosophical, 9, 121, 132;
pseudoproblem, 3, 8, 10, 13, 106, 111
Pyrrhonian Skepticism. *See* skeptic, Pyrrhonian

rational doubt, 8, 10–13; and dissolutions of the problems, 106, 109–114; and skepticism, 126–127, 129–132; Chisholm's particularism and, 85; definition of, 9; in Mercier's solution, 48; in Rescher's system, 63
Rawls, John, 99, 131
reflective equilibrium, 99, 100, 119, 131
Reid, Thomas, 76, 78
repudiation of a problem, 13, 106, 115
Rescher, Nicholas, 2, 3, 89, 107, 119, 133, 144; and coherence, 98, 99, 101, 102; and the modern problem, 111–113; the systems-theoretic approach of, 61–69
Russell, Bretrand, 8, 102
Ryan, Sharon, 113

Salmon, Wesley, 101
self-refutation, 20, 30, 31, 32; epistemic, 128, 131, 143; pragmatic, 31, 33–35, 37–38, 127
settle the dispute, 134, 139, 143; between Stoics and Skeptics, 18–20, 28–29, 34–38, 87; in Chisholm's analysis, 88, 89; in Mercier's account, 49; in Montaigne's account, 40–42; in Rescher's system, 63; in the ancient and modern problems, 105–115, 119–121
Sextus Empiricus, 2, 14, 61, 106, 107, 123, 130, 132; and the problem of the criterion, 17–38; Chisholm's version contrasted with, 74, 87–89; Mercier's version compared to, 44–48; Montaigne's version compared to, 38–

43; Rescher's version contrasted with, 62, 66, 69
skeptic, 1, 143; Academic, 2, 21, 25; critique of, 119–140; dogmatic, 77, 81–89, 95–100, 103, 105, 107, 112–115; Pyrrhonian, 20, 24–28, 30–35, 38–40, 43, 45, 48, 49, 66, 108, 132–133, 143
skepticism. *See* skeptic
Soames, Scott, 121
Socrates, 4, 5, 12, 21, 24, 25, 29, 30, 37
solution to a problem, 10, 13, 93, 99–101, 143; and Chisholm, 77, 82–86; and Mercier, 48; and Rescher, 62, 63, 69; and the infinite regress, 105–106; necessary and sufficient conditions for a, 11

Sosa, Ernest, 87, 93, 94, 105, 139
spinning wheel. *See* circular reasoning
Spinoza, Baruch, 81, 82, 87
Stalnaker, Robert, 5, 12, 121, 122
Stich, Stephen, 134–138
Stoic, 2, 20; contrasted with Sextus, 25–38, 66, 87, 89, 107–111, 132; philosophy, 21–24
Stoicism. *See* Stoic
Stough, Charlotte, 28
Strawson, P. F., 121, 122
supervenience: doctrine of, 94

vicious circle. *See* circular reasoning

Wason, P. C., 134
Williams, Michael, 100

About the Author

Robert Amico is an associate professor of philosophy at St. Bonaventure University. He has published several papers on epistemological issues in journals such as *Australian Journal of Philosophy* and *Philosophical Papers*. His essays have also appeared in the epistemology anthology titled *On Knowing and the Known*.